Commercializing Growth

Connecting Valuation with Management and Governance Methodologies

Jerry Schaufeld

Commercializing Growth: Connecting Valuation with Management and Governance Methodologies

Jerry Schaufeld
Ashland, MA, USA

ISBN-13 (pbk): 978-1-4842-7501-6   ISBN-13 (electronic): 978-1-4842-7502-3
https://doi.org/10.1007/978-1-4842-7502-3

Copyright © 2021 by Jerry Schaufeld

This work is subject to copyright. All rights are reserved by the Publisher, whether the whole or part of the material is concerned, specifically the rights of translation, reprinting, reuse of illustrations, recitation, broadcasting, reproduction on microfilms or in any other physical way, and transmission or information storage and retrieval, electronic adaptation, computer software, or by similar or dissimilar methodology now known or hereafter developed.

Trademarked names, logos, and images may appear in this book. Rather than use a trademark symbol with every occurrence of a trademarked name, logo, or image we use the names, logos, and images only in an editorial fashion and to the benefit of the trademark owner, with no intention of infringement of the trademark.

The use in this publication of trade names, trademarks, service marks, and similar terms, even if they are not identified as such, is not to be taken as an expression of opinion as to whether or not they are subject to proprietary rights.

While the advice and information in this book are believed to be true and accurate at the date of publication, neither the authors nor the editors nor the publisher can accept any legal responsibility for any errors or omissions that may be made. The publisher makes no warranty, express or implied, with respect to the material contained herein.

    Managing Director, Apress Media LLC: Welmoed Spahr
    Acquisitions Editor: Susan McDermott
    Development Editor: Laura Berendson
    Coordinating Editor: Jessica Vakili

Cover designed by eStudioCalamar

Distributed to the book trade worldwide by Springer Science+Business Media New York, 1 New York Plaza, New York, NY 10004. Phone 1-800-SPRINGER, fax (201) 348-4505, e-mail orders-ny@springer-sbm.com, or visit www.springeronline.com. Apress Media, LLC is a California LLC and the sole member (owner) is Springer Science + Business Media Finance Inc (SSBM Finance Inc). SSBM Finance Inc is a **Delaware** corporation.

For information on translations, please e-mail booktranslations@springernature.com; for reprint, paperback, or audio rights, please e-mail bookpermissions@springernature.com.

Apress titles may be purchased in bulk for academic, corporate, or promotional use. eBook versions and licenses are also available for most titles. For more information, reference our Print and eBook Bulk Sales web page at http://www.apress.com/bulk-sales.

Any source code or other supplementary material referenced by the author in this book is available to readers on GitHub via the book's product page, located at www.apress.com/978-1-4842-7501-6. For more detailed information, please visit http://www.apress.com/source-code.

Printed on acid-free paper

Table of Contents

About the Author vii

Acknowledgments ix

Introduction xi

Chapter 1: Introduction 1
    Growth Doesn't Stand Alone 1
    Elements of Growth: The "S" Curve Revisited 3
    Platform Technology 6
    Perspective 16

Chapter 2: Growth Rates 19
    Internal Factors 20
    External Factors 21
    Dealing with Internal and External Challenges 22
    Resources 24
    Perspective 24

Chapter 3: Global Perspective 27
    The Economist's View 27
    GDP as a Measure 28
    GDP: The Elements 29

TABLE OF CONTENTS

    Currency Fluctuations 31
    The Political Intrusion 32
    Other Considerations 33
    Perspective 35

Chapter 4: Strategy and Business Models 37
    Strategy... 38
    Metrics 39
    Execution 40
    Models 41

Chapter 5: Organizational Impact and Corporate Culture 43

Chapter 6: Resource Acquisition 51

Chapter 7: Allocation of Resources 65

Chapter 8: Market and Branding Considerations 71
    Framework... 71

Chapter 9: Capital/Financial Considerations 75

Chapter 10: The Role of Technology 85
    Protection... 87
    Investment 89
    Innovation and Culture 90

Chapter 11: Risks and Their Mitigation 93
    External Risks and Mitigation 94

Chapter 12: Summary... 97

Appendix A: Before You Initiate, Investigate 99
Introduction 99
A Framework to Investigate, Then Initiate 101
Case Study: Better Place 102
Conclusion 103
References 104

Index 107

About the Author

Jerry Schaufeld is an affiliate professor, professor of innovation, entrepreneurship, technology commercialization, and early-stage investment capital emeritus at Worcester Polytechnic Institute (WPI) Business School. For the past 15 years, he has taught at the Foisie School of Management at WPI in the area of new venture creation, innovation and entrepreneurship, technology commercialization, and the acquisition of capital in early-stage ventures. He consults for three venture capital firms and is currently doing research in the area of entrepreneurship models for universities.

In addition, he has taught graduate-level new venture dynamics in Switzerland (and other international locations, including China, Denmark, and Greece) and is currently working with a research team at the Neaman Institute at the Technion in Israel on the topic of improving the efficiency of the investment process. He is the author of *Commercializing Innovation* (Apress).

Acknowledgments

- **Ed Roberts**: A teacher and MIT Sloan professor who defined entrepreneurship through analysis actual MIT spinoffs and set the stage for my continual interest in the topic.

- **MacRea Banks**: Head of the WPI School of Management who defined technology commercialization in simple, understandable terms and hired me for my first teaching assignment.

- **Fourth grade teachers in Sterling, MA**: Dedicated teachers who practiced teaching excellence and provided the basis of my teaching perspective.

- **Bob McCray**: Founder of Worcester Controls and director of my company (Phoenix Controls). His quiet, authoritative "can do" attitude steered us through multiple operating issues.

- **Fabienne Miller**: A colleague who believed that teaching accounting was more than understanding arcane accounting terms.

- **Rico Baldegger**: Director of Swiss HEG Fribourg Business School. He demonstrated the profound value of international cooperation and teaching in multiple cultural environments.

ACKNOWLEDGMENTS

- **Shlomo Maital**: A colleague from the Neaman Institute in Israel. Cooperation of the potential of the "Startup Economy" in Israel with multiple initiatives at the Technion.

And of course, my beloved wife, **Sue**, who has been my support, source of caring, and a curious, energetic reader/proofreader throughout.

Introduction

The world of emerging commercial entities is accelerating at a breathtaking pace. Dimensions of modern commerce include rapidly emerging enabling technologies, Internet speed communications, and international market developments, to name a few. Impact on emerging companies presents a new set of opportunities and a chance to achieve the new attributes of being nimble and adaptive. It also allows us to execute strategies that were not available to us before.

Beyond the commercial changes, there is a new need for a means of ascertaining value propositions of the entities. The author argues the valuation dialogue should enter the board room agenda on a regular basis. To do so, new tools and the metrics to measure the changes must be developed. The purpose of the corporate model is to create shareholder involvement and thus allow measurement of the changes in value on a regular basis.

This is certainly not a local or domestic issue. Internationally, value, growth, and its measurement are being debated. An example is given in Appendix A of this book which has been contributed by two colleagues, Shlomo Maital and Eliezer Shein, from the Neaman Public Policy Institute of the Technion in Haifa, Israel. It attempts to define a "checklist" for the process of articulating the process.

The importance of value-based organizational models and the need for both dialogue and the development of the tools needed to engage that discussion led me to write this book. I hope you find it useful and that the topics of growth and valuation cause you to engage them in your organizations.

CHAPTER 1

Introduction

Growth Doesn't Stand Alone

Corporate growth is a metric marker for measuring the overall viability of an organization. This idea applies to both service-oriented and manufactured hard goods entities. There are common elements to each. Sales is a good marker for the journey. A law firm might refer to this as "billable hours," while a manufacturer might measure numbers of "units sold." Whatever the measure, it doesn't stand alone. It is not a singular measure but reflects all elements of a given organization. It has positive and negative aspects. The need for growth becomes more relevant as we move to models of increased global commerce, competition for resources, viability of talent, and the availability of capital.

Yet, despite its importance, there seems to be little agreement about central measurement metrics. The formal science of valuation first comes into focus. In its basic form, it is an actuarial synthesis that attempts to monetize all aspects of the value of corporate entities. Valuation embraces both internal and external issues. Today, its applications are on financial transactions such as raising capital and options pricing. It establishes monetary values of transactions. It is a separate field of professional endeavor that is versed in actuarial science.

CHAPTER 1   INTRODUCTION

In reviewing 12 annual reports of Fortune 500 companies, I was struck by the number of perspectives that reference growth. Some examples include

- Growth of market share
- Growth in forecast earning
- Growth in sales forecasts
- Growth in the number of patents applied for
- Growth of new market opportunities

It appears that growth per se is a marker that is prevalent to the discourse of commercial entities. Yet

- How much of a connection is there of the concept of growth to the commercial working of the entity?
- Are there stated limits to the growth potential of an organization?
  - If so, what are they… and what can be done to mitigate them?
  - Are there both upper and lower limits to the rate of growth?
- Where does the responsibility for growth lie? Who in the governance model is responsible?
- Will the new tools of analytics and simulation impact the execution of growth strategies?

In this book we will examine these issues from the perspective of the connection of them to the commercial viability of the firm. In all this activity, there is little attention to the overall measures of value which is the core of a company's existence. That connection applies to both manufacturing and services industries. In addition, not-for-profit organizations will be viewed in this context. They will be examined in both

CHAPTER 1   INTRODUCTION

their internal and external dynamics and their impact on the future growth potential of the entity. The question of how to move valuation to a viable and regular agenda item in the Board's assessment of activity is a central theme and needs to be a subject of focus. To look at growth as part of a continual process, it is useful to revisit the "S" Curve.

Elements of Growth: The "S" Curve Revisited

The "S" Curve is a graphic relationship of an entity (or project) of financial value versus time. It is called an "S" Curve because of its shape (see Figure 1-1). The curve is also referred to as sigmoidal, which is a mathematical interpretation of how the data is derived. Whatever the basis, it is a useful tool to understand where the growth elements are and thus serves as a useful measurement of progress to prescribed goals. The representation in Figure 1-1 is focused on the financial perspective.

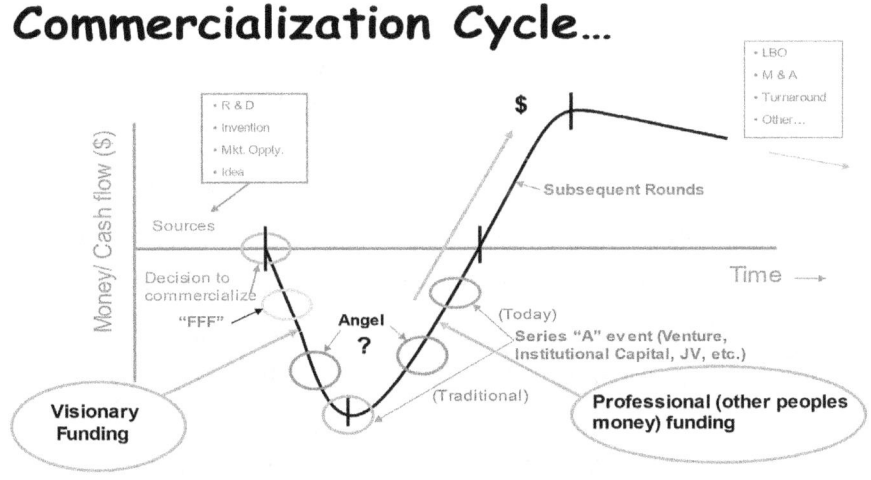

Figure 1-1. The "S" Commericalization Curve

3

CHAPTER 1 INTRODUCTION

There are three major domains in the "S" Curve life cycle. They include

- Development of the ideas, devices (or services), and supporting finance and/organizations
- The launch and growth segment, which includes measurements, strategy, and implementation skills
- The maturity phase where opportunities to extend the curves lie
- Further details about the curve's elements include the following perspectives:
  - The first is the *investment phase* where various elements of preparing an entity or project occurs. Prototypes, IP, teams, and marketing strategies are created here. It is shown as a negative slope because there is no offsetting source(s) of revenue(s) available.
  - As the product (or service) is launched, a *period of growth* is defined. After the startup costs are recovered, the model might also portray profit growth at this time. The implications of surpassing (or missing) growth objectives which can be seen at this stage of the graph are portrayed.
  - The third element of this figure is the *maturity phase* in which aging technology, diminishing market presence, changing organizational focus, or simply competitive forces challenge the growth phase shown in the second part of the graph.

The entering part of the "S" Curve is portrayed as a negative slope as it reflects those expenditures (and time) required to launch a product

CHAPTER 1   INTRODUCTION

or service. This segment is characterized by expenditures without offsetting revenue. It is also a time when both professional investors and non-equity sources (banks) are least interested. This quandary is resolved by informal sources of capital ranging from credit cards to friends, family, and fools (referred to as "F, F, and F"), early-stage Angel groups, and even some small venture funds. It is also a time where non-equity dilutive forms such as government grants (e.g., SBIR grants) should be considered. Certainly, money/capital is key issue, but other resources such as people (organizational development) and technology, including secured intellectual property (IP), are also required... yet the models are fragile enough to not directly support them. Acquisition of resources will be discussed later in the text in a more detailed manner.

The external focus in this phase is the "launch" of products (or services) which allows sources of revenue from sales transactions to be used to offset the stream of early-stage developmental expenses. It also is the beginning of the realization of the growth potential segment of the entity's life cycle.

In this phase there are a variety of new conditions that must be encountered such as the following:

a. Is the product or service scalable?

b. Are there enough product elements to confront competition and changing market influences? The analogy that a company can fly "under the radar" until the growth phase certainly applies.

c. Are there enough internal resources of technology, IP, capital availability, organizational depth, and market savvy to confront the issues of growth?

d. Is the technology platform broad enough to allow multiple paths and features?

CHAPTER 1   INTRODUCTION

    e. Is there intellectual property to sustain a market place position?

    f. Is the organization savvy enough to reinvent itself during the various phases of growth?

    g. Are the BOD and C-level teams deep and agile enough to anticipate and resolve issues of growth management?

What becomes intriguing is the rate of change in these conditions and how many variations occur to make it work. Attributes like being nimble and adaptive become increasingly important. Certainly, good planning skills contribute much to a successful outcome. Later we will look at forward planning in detail. "What if" becomes a useful tool to sort out directions to go and selection of adequate resources.

One example of this lies in the realm of technical competence. What may have been an adequate platform in the early stages of growth may not be adequate for future directions. An array of possibilities presents themselves.

Platform Technology

The "S" Curve is usually presented as a singular line or transfer function. This helps identify the areas of slope change in the life cycle of either a product or organizational entity. It also misses the possibilities of alternate strategies for growth.

Some time you might want to try the following experiment. In a new car, open the hood. You might observe open space on the fire wall. If you were to ask a local mechanic, "What is that space for?," they might say that it is a space reserved for next year's model when a new feature for the succeeding model will use it. That level of platform design/marketing sophistication protects capital investment, design, and engineering resources... and is mostly invisible to the user.

Another example is a modern high-density computer chip. Inside might be layers after layer of densely packed components, but only a small portion is enabled or used at introduction. The rest might be stored for future iteration. The invested "foundry" costs of creating a modern chip can run into billions of dollars. Platform design technology allows those costs to be spread over multiple years and applications. This concept can be seen graphically in Figure 1-2.

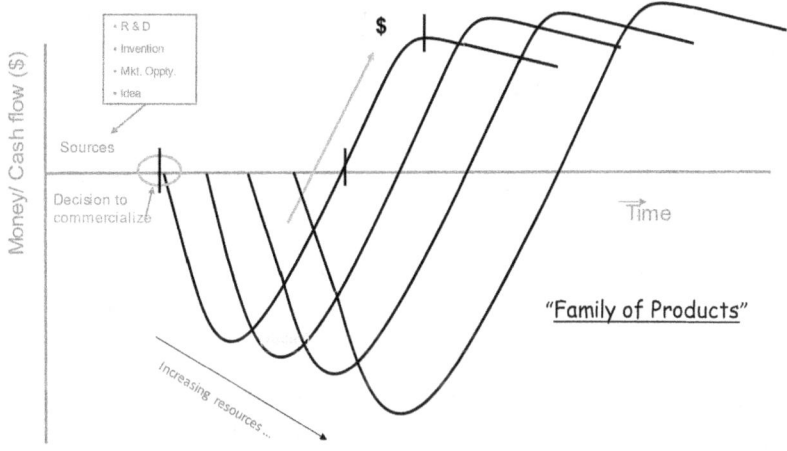

Figure 1-2. *Family of Products Strategy*

Although the value of this approach can be seen both intuitively and empirically, it is not without issues and risks. Some considerations include

- Dilution of central focus/vision of the entity
- Inadequate financial and internal resources to achieve multiple paths

7

CHAPTER 1   INTRODUCTION

- Confusion of brand identity
- Inadequate market capacity
- Improper internal skills and capital equipment structure
- Unknown market competition
- Other unknowns

Each of these considerations can be confronted.

Central Focus. It is increasingly important that those entities that articulate clear-cut visions fare better than those who don't. Allocation of both human and financial resources becomes more accurate. Tactical directional decisions become more articulate and clearly stated. This allows individuals who have the responsibility of implementing them to be more effective in executing their responsibilities.

Several years ago, I had the opportunity to visit the headquarters of Ben & Jerry's located in central Vermont. For non-New Englanders, Ben & Jerry's is high-quality ice cream with mostly regional distribution. In their central manufacturing facility, one can observe the three tenets of their vision, which is focused on three elements which are painted on the walls in bold letters. They include Economic Mission, Social Mission, and Product Mission. With a small sign on wall, visitors are encouraged to ask any employee to articulate the three elements. I did and found that a basic employee pushing material cart through the plant could not only articulate the three elements, but could expound on what they meant to him doing his job. Wow.

Resources for Growth. The planning for and acquisition of resources for a growth enterprise is an art form. The forecast models must rely on assumptions that can change rapidly, and the penalty of error is magnified.

CHAPTER 1   INTRODUCTION

If one or more of the multiple resources required lags, the other attributes of growth are stifled. Let's look at a few key elements:

- **Human Resources:** Acquiring both the quantity and quality of appropriate experience and skills is a demanding task. Quickly individual personal contacts are exploited and the hard (and expensive) pursuit in the marketplace begins. Perhaps the most critical of these is the time constant it takes of identifying people, acquiring their services, and then positioning them in a changing organization to be effective. Yikes... any of the three would be daunting enough. Many projects fail simply because they don't have the organizational structure and depth required to accomplish their growth objectives.

- **Capital:** Financial capital and the structure of fixed assets can be strong building blocks for an organization. Capital structure plays an important dimension in at least two ways. When capital is depleted, all elements of growth stop. Simply, the absence of working capital is a primary reason for a project or business failure. Most "other" elements such as markets, people, and technology can be acquired. There is a finality to the end of cash. Preparing for liquid asset acquisition such as cash requires detailed planning, a path to sources of capital, and effective construct such as a detailed business plan.

- **Technology:** To many of my technically savvy colleagues, there is a sense that technology is a finite entity to be simply exploited in the marketplace. Where it so simple? Reality tells us that the engineering

9

CHAPTER 1 INTRODUCTION

aspects of a product must be viewed as a continuum of change. Each element must be understood and properly utilized in the life cycle of a product or service. One starting point is the acquisition of intellectual property (IP) support. In the art form of patent applications is the carefully constructed set of claims that envision the full life cycle of the idea.

The federal government provides a 20-year monopoly protection of an idea through the issue of patents (or copyrights, as applicable). Patents can be shared by licensing in both outgoing and inbound applications. Certain industries such as pharmaceuticals rely heavily on IP because of the long (and expensive) development cycles. One alternative to securing IP is to maintain a proprietary safeguard of the ideas that govern a given technology. There is a somewhat public story about the Cambridge, MA-based Polaroid Corporation (developers of chemical-based instant photography). At one point, they employed almost 16,000 technically skilled workers. Only three of them knew the full process of photo development cycle. Another commercial example is Coca-Cola. The formula for original drink is guarded in a huge safe in the basement of their corporate headquarters in Atlanta, GA. Amazing for sure.

Organization. Of all the parts of the puzzle of organizational growth, governance issues are both the least understood and yet have the potential for the most impact on the successful (and unsuccessful) outcomes of growth initiatives. To begin to understand this paradox, it might be important to look at how the corporate model is presented. A traditional organization chart might be envisioned as shown in Figure 1-3.

CHAPTER 1   INTRODUCTION

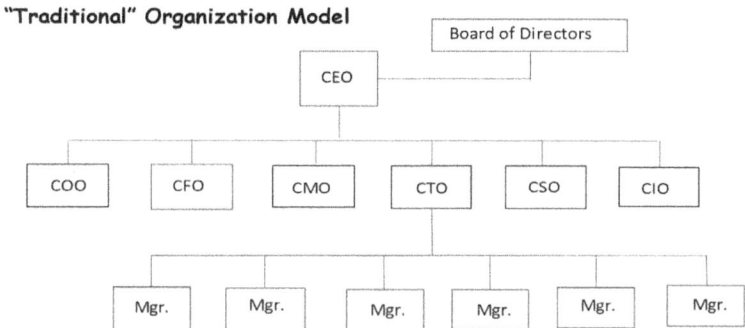

Figure 1-3. *Traditional Organizational Model*

This visual representation suggests that the model is hierarchal and the span is finite. Traditionally, a governing Board of Directors oversees the operations. In a narrow definition, they have a fiduciary responsibility to the shareholders of the entity. They manage the performance of the Chief Executive Officer (CEO) and oversee the C-level performance. In additional they approve the significant financial operations that include long-term capital expenditures and operating budgets.

Folklore then has it that organizational models should not be wider that six reports. The "Rule of Six" has been attributed to IBM for their management work in the 1950 era. Today it is common belief that the Rule of Six allows organizations to perform in a more nimble and adaptive fashion to market conditions. Those attributes are held in high value today. Later in this text, we will explore some of the inner workings of how the organizational structures contribute to the growth of an organization in detail.

Marketing (and Sales). The growth potential for a given project or entity relies on an understanding of who the customer is, how they buy, and the demographics surrounding them. Some of the market-centered issues are as follows:

- Where is the customer located?
- What are the spending habits and financial capacity of a potential buyer to achieve them?

11

CHAPTER 1 INTRODUCTION

- What are the competitive forces surrounding that purchase decision?
- What external issues (i.e., regulatory) impact the buying decision?
- What are the follow-on opportunities of the sale?

These are some of the perspectives surrounding the market definitions for a product or service. Most important is that a plan of action to achieve the sales success be created. It is called a marketing plan. It should contain measurable metrics to monitor the path into the market opportunity. Further, if the marketing function is a partner in product development, it increases the probability of a successful outcome.

The marketing function is not connected to the sales function. They are distinctly separate. Confusion and misuse of funding resources escalate when the two functions are connected. One exception might be a company's presence at a trade show. Although the participation at the show is in the domain of marketing, sales personnel can actually work in the show booth and interact with the potential customers.

External Issues/Competition. Beyond the internal resource allocation matter, there is a significant number of external issues that challenge a given firm's growth objectives. Competition come to mind early. It is driven by another firm's observations that the very conditions that make a project attractive may also appeal to others. A competitor's offering can either be as good as the project envisioned or they can be better/worse. Feature characteristics are certainly important. Pricing becomes a constant threat. It can impact both gross margins and profit. The arena of feature/benefits can be one of intense competition. An example is the automobile rental business. Avis and Hertz have been ferocious competitors for years. It is difficult to distinguish their offerings in the marketplace. Joint ventures offer an enticing alternative to direct competition.

CHAPTER 1   INTRODUCTION

External Issues/Other. There are a wide range of other external issues beyond competition that any project encounters. There are broad regulations and laws that range from antitrust to tax limitations, accounting rules, industry standards, safety regulations, OSHA, and other safety regulations, to name a few. It is not uncommon to create a position of compliance officer to assure that those rules that impact growth are being maintained. Certain industries such as pharmaceutical manufacturing and aircraft production are heavily regulated for health or safety reasons. Those industries prove that external regulation can be confronted and managed. That it increases internal costs is for certain. The balance comes from the fact that all companies in a given industry are confronted with the same issues. It levels the playing fields.

Most times the external and regulatory issues are delineated in the risk section of a business plan. What is not interesting is the presence of those risks, but rather that the plan indicates methods for confronting and mitigating them.

Post-sales Opportunities. Beyond the original sales transaction between a supplier and customer, there lies an opportunity for additional follow-on work and its commensurate revenue and profit. The significant cost of finding and securing a customer is the most expensive part of the sales cycle. Imagine if there were follow-on work with same costumer. There are certainly many opportunities.

A project manager at Johnson Controls (Fortune 500 company) told me that on a given controls project, they see about 35% possibilities for additional work. In addition, the gross margin contribution that works could be as high as 80%. In the Johnson Controls case, they have been known to secure follow-on work as trivial as maintaining the property to assure continuity and follow-on opportunities. We are all familiar with extended warranty contracts, discounts on future sales, and discounted service contracts in the day-to-day commercial transactions in which we participate.

13

CHAPTER 1   INTRODUCTION

Disruption. Clayton Christensen, a renowned professor at the Harvard Business School, wrote a book entitled *The Innovator's Dilemma*. In that text, he promulgated that for growth to occur, there had to be changes in the marketplace and/or product offering that were considered "disruptive." Disruptive innovation became the mantra for high growth and positive change in organizations.

There were four elements to his formula for successful innovative disruption. They include

- That the companies already have innovative trajectories that continue for years. They were coined "sustaining innovation." They featured incremental improvements in profit margins, market penetration into existing markets, and modest changes in technology. (He cites the automotive industry with annual increases in fuel efficiency and horsepower.)

- A second observation is that pace of sustaining innovation along an established trajectory outstrips the customer's ability to use it. He cites the introduction of personal computers transitions to word processing where typist had to commonly stop to allow the prevalent Intel 286 processors to catch up to the inputs. Today, that is not the case.

- Christensen points out that mangers can respond to change but fail to exploit the opportunities they present. Resource allocation of projects that can support change is woefully short. That allows projects and services that are not as good as those in the market to languish. Of course, this also opens the door to competitive forces that can exploit this weakness and make progress in each market.

CHAPTER 1   INTRODUCTION

- Incumbents can flounder as a result of disruptive technologies that have the potential to improve existing product's performance but aren't implemented. The consequences of this can be a failure that is exploited by competitors. The examples he cites could have been corrected, but the behavior of the incumbents is the primary cause of this nonperformance. When reading this section, I couldn't help reflecting on the example of the automotive industry and the evolution of hybrid propulsion technology. Detroit has the largest capacity in the world to innovate and build cars in the world. Yet, in 2019 the hybrid vehicles' disruptive entry into the market was managed by Japanese sources. Today, about 500 thousand hybrid vehicles are sold in the United States annually.

To step back from this, it becomes apparent that there is sustaining value to bold and disruptive change. Incremental change may have a redeeming value in product or market extensions, but it does not deliver long-term sustainable growth opportunities. It also utilizes human, technical, material, and financial resources while delivering only marginal returns. Assurances to sustain directions in long-term growth that come from strong governance directions including the Board, C-level management, and alert operational decision-making become predominant.

The Digital Economy. So much of the attention to the dynamics of growth is attached to the space of the digital economy. It does not mean that large capital investment industries (i.e., steel mills) aren't innovative or disruptive... but, they pall when compared to the rates of change in the nimbler digital economies. In a recent SAE Journal (2017) article on automotive use of microprocessors, it was estimated that a modern automobile utilizes about 20 microprocessors. High-end cars use more to control their luxury features. Their applications range from engine and

CHAPTER 1   INTRODUCTION

driving to controls to entertainment and GPS systems. The breathtaking rise of chip functionality per application, enormous decline in memory consumption, and ensuing power consumption allow the chips to be "embedded" in their applications. The bewildering array of sensors, diagnostics, service, and cost reductions extends their reach into common appliances and products. Imagine a home door lock that features both a camera and security systems at competitive prices. Yikes.

The Entrepreneurial Mindset. Several years ago, I was principal investigator of a grant sponsored by the Kern Family Foundation in Milwaukee. The foundation's mission was to instill the "entrepreneurial mindset" into the perspective of engineers. The foundation (located in Waukegan, Wisconsin) was formed by Mr. Robert Kern and his wife, Mrs. Pat Kern. Mr. Kern was an engineer who among other things was curious about two cycle internal combustion engines. He formed the Generac Holdings to manufacture and sell backup electrical power supplies and machines that use two cycle engines as one of its alternate power supplies.

One arm of the foundation is called the Kern Entrepreneurial Engineering Network (KEEN). KEEN's goal was to (a) disseminate information among its member schools and (b) provide a "workshop" space for them to practice their findings. In addition, it offered grants to promote those ideas into practice.

Perspective

Transactions have been the backbone of civilized commercial activity. In the very early days, even the primitive exchanges and barters of the cavemen included both expressed and non-expressed elements. Even in the imagined barter of a piece of firewood for a piece of meat, it was assumed that the firewood would burn and meat would be edible.

Absurdly simple... maybe. Today we have array of increasingly complex transactions that have both stated and unstated expectations. In this book we will focus on an array of early-stage business interactions and how both the stated and unstated expectations affect both the ongoing activities surrounding the interaction, but even more important how we can use that knowledge to improve the outcomes of these activities.

If it were as simple as just looking at the dialogue of the principles, that would be great. Layered above the back-and-forth of the principles are levels of customs, laws, regulations, and industry standards. When the discussion is ratcheted up to the global perspective, the surrounding issues reach a significant complexity. Growth is central to all these efforts.

The concept of growth is central to commerce. It is not alone, but it impacts many elements of the measure of success of an entity. Let's look at a few elements:

- Valuation is a measure of the worth of an asset or a company today (and in the future) (James Chen, Investopedia, April 18, 2019). There is some controversy about how to measure valuation, where the consistently and comparative nature over time is valuable. The three major measures of valuation include
    - Capital structure, including debt, risk, and growth capacity
    - Analysis of future earnings
    - Market value
- Cash flow
- Human resources
- Market presence
- Operational efficiency

CHAPTER 1   INTRODUCTION

Maybe not a complete list, but certainly it is representative of the many ways the issues of growth impact an ongoing enterprise. Simply stated, growth does not stand alone. Sometimes it is envisioned within the profile of a normal maturity of an organization. In the subsequent chapters, we will examine the elements in more detail and see their importance to the value of growth.

CHAPTER 2

Growth Rates

There are multiple metrics of growth in each organization. In combination, they present a perspective for the future performance of a project or corporate entity. Multiple factors control the growth rates and perceived performance against the goals they envision. To understand the multiple (and sometimes competing) influences on growth, we will look at both the internal and external forces.

An example might be the measurement of sales growth. Typically, it is measured by changes in revenue. Sometimes it is measured by changes in the number of customers and/or their demographic mix. Yet, most sales-related metrics are resolved in gross margin contributions. Whatever method is employed, internal rewards for performance metrics such as bonuses and group recognition are utilized to continue that behavior.

Without the integration of all functions to the growth metric, a flawed model of the overall entity is displayed. The implications are significant in that any one functional area can scuttle even the best of plans. A new set of overall measurements are required.

Sometimes it seems as though current metrics are likened to taxi meter which records the accumulated expenses of a given trip. Some of the more modern ones even calculate the total trip remaining. Unfortunately, corporate metrics do not have an analogous tool.

CHAPTER 2 GROWTH RATES

Internal Factors

These influences are observed first. They are easier to control and allow for trade-offs within the organization. Factors include the following:

- There are a multitude of opportunities for control of growth within an organization. They are roughly contained in the areas of governance and management control. Governance embraces the roles of the Board of Directors, top management (the CEO), and C-level management. In theory, the Board exists at the call of the shareholders. Financial gains attributed to growth certainly are accrued to them. Operationally, the Board controls financial capital expenditures, acquisition of resources including raising money, and the behavior of the CEO through proper goal setting and performance rewards for prescribed behavior. Accurate information flow is required to assure that this governance model works in concert with the organization.

- Technology influences occur both internally and externally. It is interesting to observe the change in internal research and development (R and D) efforts. On Route 1 in New Jersey, the architecture was dominated by impressive facilities of the companies who dominated Central New Jersey. Those facilities have all but disappeared. Dynamics in technology development whereby advances progress are continually accelerating and are less dependent on significant facilities. Certainly, there are exceptions. Steel mills, by their very nature, rely on huge facilities. The Homer Research Laboratories of Bethlehem Steel dominated the landscape of their hometown of

Bethlehem, PA. In 2005, the campus which had been coined "the greatest steel research facility in the world" was closed. The balance of maintaining intellectual property protection plays an important role in assuring a robust technological leadership.

- Of all the resources required to grow a company or a project, the financial capacity to support short-term liquidity and longer capital outlays of the project rises to an early priority. Weakness in the financial capacity of project is the primary basis for failure. It is likened to an airplane or automobile that runs out of fuel – it simply stops. Fuel or cash starvation is unnecessary consequence. Proper planning, careful acquisition, and distribution of financial controls allow for the proper outcome. It takes a forward vision, care, and certainly discipline that are critical.

External Factors

There are multiple influences outside the immediate control management of a given project or surrounding organization… yet, they have the potential to significantly alter the outcomes. Some elements include the following:

- Perhaps the most dynamic attribute to be considered is within the space of marketing. It embraces competitive pressures and changes in prevailing demographics and economics, to name a few. Required are the new metrics of marketing which include being nimble to change and implementing adaptive strategies. Critical to the success of this functional domain is the integration to technology and customer needs.

- Beyond the direct impact of market adaptations, there are a realm of secondary influences such as regulatory changes and safety workplace rules (i.e., OSHA). In addition, cross-country cultural changes (i.e., currency fluctuations) and international country agreements can present both opportunities and significant challenges to the outcomes. As we become increasingly global-centric, these considerations become closer to stage center and certainly cannot be ignored.

- Marketing is first a gathering of information about customers and potential ones. It gathers age, gender, education, income status, and others. The purpose is to allow the marketing (professionals) user to synthesize the demographic information and then to allocate the programs that guide the ensuing sales effort. Clarity between the disciplines and their responsivities is crucial.

Dealing with Internal and External Challenges

With this preliminary list of internal and external issues in front of us, there becomes a challenge of how to best deal with them. What is so striking is that most of the issues are both predictable and preventable. Fundamental planning, simulations of outcomes, allocation of resources, and nimble management are part of the successful outcomes. Let's look at the elements in more detail:

- There is a balance between disruptive and incremental changes. In the spectrum of these two limits are an array of different dynamics. The weighted average of their collective actions becomes the number upon which the effort can be measured.

CHAPTER 2   GROWTH RATES

- The positive tension of the countervailing forces that control the growth performance resides in the governance balance of the project. This direction is sometimes overlooked, but the Board should participate in long-term decisions about business and long-term expenditures in a delightful balance that doesn't interfere with daily operations. Selections of Board members becomes critical. Membership should embrace core business and market knowledge as well as control of the central management. In my company each member had an "assignment" of areas of expertise on which we relied. The older model of "friends at the county club" is no longer valid. At the more tactical level, the influence that the Board can have at C level can becomes a delicate power balance that must be managed. Board-level interference should not be tolerated.

- There are many platforms that allow for successful implementation of tactical growth strategies. They include:

    - Focus of vision and goals rises to the top of the list. It provides for alignment between the goals and the actual tasks that are required to implement them. Offsite workshops and use of professional facilitators rise to the top of the list.

    - Budget definition allows for allocation of resources that are consistent with the overall goals.

    - Finally, timely reporting and bidirectional information flow and measurable reporting are paramount to successful results.

CHAPTER 2   GROWTH RATES

Resources

The acquisition and allocation of resources within a given project or company become the primary focus of its management. Some of the areas of priority include the following:

- Capital formation and its disbursement: This includes near-term expense management and longer-term capital investment.
- Talent acquisition and its deployment.
- Capital management such a real estate manufacturing equipment and distribution scenarios.
- Management of resources related to long-term strategic goals and coordination with governance directions.
- Cash management rises high in scale of prioritization — almost any other resource can be supplemented. Lack of cash represents closure and/or disbandment.

Depending on the business area a firm is in, the nature of the list changes. The capital intensity of steel mill, for example, is quite different than a software or service endeavor.

Perspective

The central point of all measurements becomes the need to have a measurable set of metrics that both reflect the current state of business and also allow indicators of future protentional opportunities and possible issues. There are techniques about measurement that are embraced in the disciplines of valuation. Today, the disciplines of valuation occur at moments of financial transactional activity.

When initial capitalization of an entity occurs, the challenge of assessing the value becomes difficult. There is simply not enough data to support the logic of analyzing the entity. Investors tend to use benchmark data from similar pricing scenarios. There are alternatives where discounts against future transactions occur. Parsing out stock ownership against discounted vestment schedules also helps defer the pressure of valuation of early-stage projects.

As companies process their way on the growth cycle ("S" Curve), there are events that occur that require some form of valuation exercise. Pricing of options and changes in personal life scenario (death, divorce, etc.) all require some form of assessment of worth. Transactions such as joint ventures, mergers, or even equity liquidations all call on valuation disciplines. Of course, endgame liquidations of the total enterprise call into effect the analysis of valuation.

Maybe this isn't the best use of valuation disciplines. Why shouldn't it be brought in force on a regular basis? Perhaps, the agenda of board meetings should include regular, disciplined analysis. Today, that is not the case. But there is a compelling argument for its inclusion on a regular basis while there is still time (and resources) to alter the outcomes.

CHAPTER 3

Global Perspective

Corporate entities, partnerships, and other business models operate in structures dominated by hierarchal governance (Boards), management, and worker/professional staff. Yet influences on the operating goals performance today reach global perspectives. In this chapter, we will look at those influences. They can be both positive and negative… but they cannot be ignored.

Among the understandings of how these outside influences impact a given organization is an acknowledgment of the shrinking aspect of these environments. Interconnections of commerce, the Internet, financial fluidity, and the speed in which these transactions occur are increasingly interrelated. Probably in the implementation of these influences, the Internet overwhelms other considerations. Its increased speed and interconnectivity make us wonder where this capacity can go. We will examine how the various functional elements of the operations are affected singularly and in total. It is a fascinating journey.

The Economist's View

There is a prevailing view that global economic growth is declining. In her article published in the Stanford Business School Journal (November 22, 2019) entitled "Uncertainty Drags Down Global Growth," May Wong, a scholar, observes that "uncertainty about economic trends will have a chilling impact on business." The element she cites includes tariffs and trade policy.

CHAPTER 3   GLOBAL PERSPECTIVE

In his paper entitled "The Economies Adding the Most to Global Growth in 2019" (Visual Capitalist, 2019), Jeff Desjardins points out the following trends in GDP growth (see Figure 3-1). The annual decline over 10 years is significant.

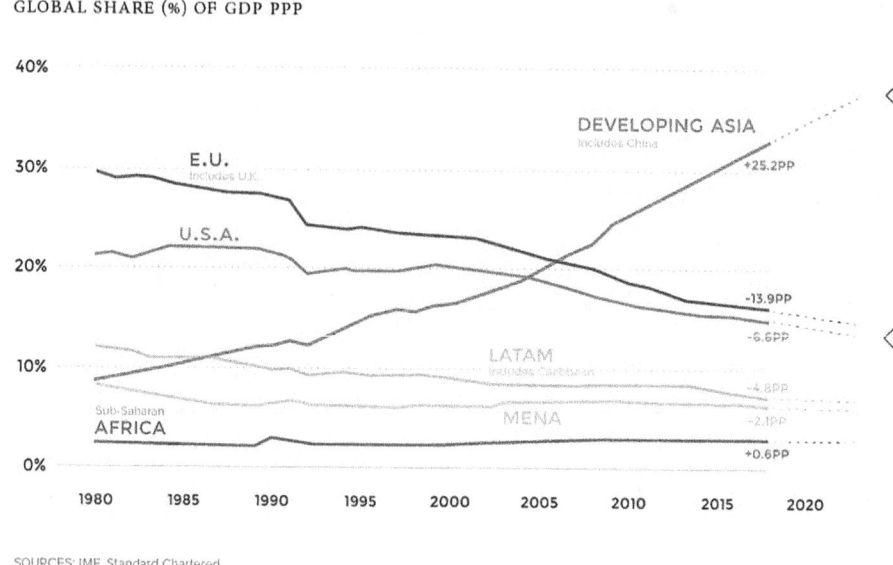

Figure 3-1. Global GDP Share

Of interest is the observation that the two leading contributors, the United States and European Union, are in decline. The rise of Asia is noted but is compromised today by tariffs and local economies in transition.

GDP as a Measure

To achieve a perspective on growth about business, one must first understand the economist's need for understanding the magnitude of changes in the national environments of participating countries. Later in this text, we will see the linkages of macroeconomics to individual

CHAPTER 3   GLOBAL PERSPECTIVE

companies and projects. An agreed upon tool was the gross domestic product (GDP).

Developed by Simon Kuznets in 1934, the GDP attempts to monetize economic production of individuals, companies, and the government. Kuznets was an economist who received the 1971 Nobel Prize in Economic Sciences for his work that linked empirical science to quantitative economic history (Investopedia, December 2019, Dotsdale Publishing).

GDP has endured as a basic reference for national economic measurement. It is comprised of three perspectives which include the monetary value of expenditures, production, and incomes. It is usually adjusted for inflation and price changes. There are multiple measurement tools, but only the GDP has endured. Significant attention is given to changes in GDP as an indication of either growth or decline. It also serves as a comparative measure between countries to compare advances and declines.

GDP: The Elements

Although GDP is the basic measure of national growth, there are several adjustments that must be considered. The raw data that comprises the GDP is called the nominal GDP. Considerations for inflation (both additive and subtractive) are then considered. It is then called the real GDP. From this both annual and quarterly calculations are derived and used to establish growth rates and per capita assessments. One powerful application of these measurements is that the balance of trade between nations can then be derived. From this, various international economic incentives, tariffs, and taxes can be established. It's powerful, and as we can see later in this book, it has direct bearing on the economic well-being of individual companies.

Macroeconomic indicators can only take decision trends so far. They are certainly useful for time period comparison (i.e., year to year), but they don't directly help with specific corporation-level decision-making. They

CHAPTER 3 GLOBAL PERSPECTIVE

require more detail to do that. Some examples of next-level indicators utilized by The Conference Board (January 30, 2020 report) are

- Stock market indexes
- Gold futures
- New order (consumer and manufacturing)
- Building permits
- Weekly jobless claims

Their forecasts are usually comprised of a series of ten indicators presented as a composite number called the Conference Board Leading Economic Index. It is published monthly. There is still another level of information that is shown in composite indexes. Lumber, for instance, is a volatile commodity that demonstrates changes in its composite pricing. NASDAQ provides the data shown in Figure 3-2.

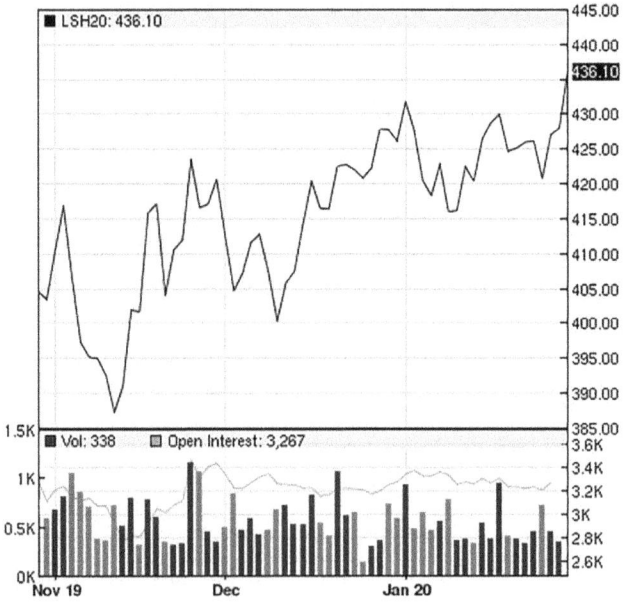

Figure 3-2. Lumber index (Nasdaq, 2020)

If you were a furniture manufacturing company, the global indices might be of interest to your business strategy. Lumber price fluctuations in a remote country can affect a company's manufacturing profitability and even the selection of product offerings they might produce. But there is more.

Currency Fluctuations

Beyond specific markers such as lumber prices for the earlier cited hypothetical furniture manufacturer, there are monetary changes that cannot be ignored because they sweep across multiple industries. They are in the area of currency fluctuations. Historically, money exchange rates were anchored to a gold standard. It had the result that fluctuations in currency value was somewhat stable. There were changes in that gold was no longer the standard and countries began to use floating standards where a variety of internal indices became the basis for a country's setting the value of currency. Some of the factors considered were

- National economic activity
- A country's growth rate
- Interest rates
- Geopolitical risk

The impact of these fluctuations is to create uncertainty in the value of money over time. If a long-term–based capital equipment expenditure, a market-based external transaction, or simple growth investment is being considered, the cost of the capital becomes uncertain and thus difficult to compute. In simpler terms, the cost of money becomes uncertain. The longer the time period of the investment, the more difficult it is to understand its outcome.

CHAPTER 3   GLOBAL PERSPECTIVE

Beyond long-term capital considerations, short-term fluctuations impact the sale and flow of international merchandise and services. An international sales transaction price is fixed, but the currency exchange at the time of the transaction may differ. This leads to adjustment and discounts. Accounting standards allow for reserve funds to buffer these changes, but this is only within specified ranges. It can be argued that these changes ebb and flow in such a way that the fluctuations cancel each other. Long-term data refutes this, but in a short term, there might be neutral offsets.

The Political Intrusion

If we circle back to the (hypothetical) furniture maker who relies on external sources of lumber to both run and grow his business, we might look at some of the geopolitical forces upon which they have no control:

- A local municipality near the rain forest implements restrictions on what trees can be harvested in the nearby forest.
- One or more government established tariffs on offshore wood imported into a given country change.
- When environmentalists prevail, certain elements of the wood production cycle are forbidden.
- A generalized strike occurs in one of the West Coast ports where offshore wood enters this country and throttles the supply chain for raw materials.

How does the furniture maker or any ongoing business entity deal with external uncertainty? There are two extremes: The first is to simply ignore these factors and pragmatically deal with the resultant. The other extreme is to agonize continually over the trends and changes they represent. Where is the middle?

Certainly, a balance can be struck. In my interviews with a series of 12 operating CEOs, I did find examples of the extremes. One common path is to prioritize which economic indicators have most relevance to the ongoing business. They are not of equal impact. Each indicator has a unique time constant with respect to their impact on a given entity. Local representation in foreign environments resonated as a common success factor.

On the operating side, there is an argument for the well-capitalized organization. It can seize opportunities that are in its favor. The furniture manufacturer can build up inventories of price swings of the lumber index. This can translate into increased profitability and strategic market options in discounts that might be passed on to the consumer. Sometimes, consortiums of like industries combine their purchasing power and amplify those opportunities presented by fluctuations captured by economic indicators.

Other Considerations

Not all risks are economic and can be tracked on long-term economic indicators. Some other categories include the following:

- **Acts of God**: A series of large, lightning-caused fires of the magnitude of those that recently occurred in Australia can significantly affect the sources of lumber in the abovementioned furniture manufacturer is a good example. Similarly, floods, windstorms, and land erosion can abruptly alter the uses of raw materials. In common, they are not predictable.
- **Disruptive Innovation**: Technological improvements in materials and process equipment are accelerating rapidly. In addition, some changes are not linear

and are capable of disruptive impact. Imagine a new development of a synthetic wood material on our furniture maker.

- **Marketplace Changes**: The addition, subtraction, or combination/alliances of competitors can quickly change the market landscape. Beyond these are the unknowns and the presence of "big box" (i.e., Walmart) players. Their ability to control supply chains and even local pricing can be highly disruptive and not predictable.

- **Infrastructure Changes**: One CEO that I interviewed told me that his business viability changed abruptly when the local public works committee changed the traffic flow past his store by adding "One Way" street signs. The change had been approved by local jurisdictions and was thus justified. No one contacted him. He later appealed it and won demographics. The signs were removed.

- **Changing Demographics**: The emergence of "baby boomer" movement, the rapidly changing demographics of the newly mobile Generation X, and the explosive growth of new housing starts can have a dramatic influence on the customer population for a given entity. In addition, new municipal regulations caused by these demographic changes can have the same disruptive impact.

Perspective

Opportunity and Risk

Global indicators lie beyond the scope of a given commercial entity. Yet they can have enormous impact on the operating parameters of an ongoing operation. The same is true of environmental and demographic influences. Dealing with them certainly offers opportunities that are countered by the risk options of not confronting them. In this rapidly changing world, nimble management tactics will be most rewarded. As stated in earlier chapters, these factors must certainly be reconciled in a short-term valuation accounting as they could have significant impact on the future potential of a given entity. Today's global perspective is simply too persuasive to allow international elements to be ignored.

CHAPTER 4

Strategy and Business Models

Business strategies and ideas begin with a stated vision or goals that set the stage for moving ahead. It becomes increasingly important that the proper planning and documentation be put in place before that effort begins. The most common form of documentation is captured in a business plan format. It may be encompassed in budgets and other formal documents but in common certain issues must be articulated. They include

- Overall goals and objectives
- A delineation of resources (both human and financial) that are required
- Measurable outcomes
- Identification of risks and the plans to mitigate them
- An articulation of platforms and families of products that will sustain the growth.
- Internal benefits of growth on the remaining organization

CHAPTER 4   STRATEGY AND BUSINESS MODELS

Strategy

Strategy, as it relates to projects or companies, is a broad landscape. What is known is that those efforts that have a clear, articulated vision (or goal) that is communicated into the organizational workings have higher probability of successful outcomes. If there is one dimension to company's efforts that this idea applies, it is the area of growth. Yet, within that space there are a multitude of metrics that attempt to capture the overall growth dynamic.

One example is a growth in sales; it is a common means of speaking to the overall perspective of the project or company's performance. But does it convey the overall value of the metric? I suspect not as it only looks at one metric – not the overall project performance. If, for example, it just reported sales growth but ignored the cash position changes it took to achieve it, it becomes a disservice to the perspective of the value of an overall performance.

There is an alternative to individual measurements that deals with the overall operating parameters of the company. It is the concept of valuation. Today, valuation is used in capital acquisition projects, M and A transactions, and divestiture projects. It is also extended to family-owned company transactions to help assess the proper monetary aspects of a given situation. Why isn't it used as a more common and regular measurement?

The ownership of growth resides in the governance model of the enterprise. Members of the Board are chosen to represent the shareholder's equity position. It is a fiduciary responsibility. Yet in the perusal of twelve public companies and a series of privately owned board agendas, there is no serious discussion about ongoing valuation. There is no easy way to understand this dichotomy.

Metrics

In an enlightening article published in the *Harvard Business Review* (October 2012) entitled the "True Measures of Success," the author, Michael J. Mauboussin, argues that most companies use improper performance metrics. Either the management teams favor one set of numbers, while others may use external or industry standards. The resulting conflicting metrics skew the realization of company value objectives. Let us look at some of the common metrics to see if they will give insight as to this mismatch.

- **Revenue Growth:** A common measure of an organization's growth is the cumulative sales growth. In simple terms, it is the number of units sold times the average selling price (ASP). Even those two numbers can unravel to mask challenges of the organization's potential. For example, if ASP is altered with sales discounts and other incentives, it skews the gross revenue picture. It might also mask gross margin weaknesses such as increased material costs, increased labor (overtime)costs, and resultant challenges to the organization's ability to complete successful marketing programs as well as product development efforts.

- **Market Share Growth:** Some argue the merits of market share. In many ways it is positive in that it allows brand dominance, economic (pricing) advantages, feature control, and competitive strengths against others that will try to enter the space. On the other side, it stifles the ability of an organization to reach to other market positions in the same space. Why should a potential customer reach for new products when basic needs are satisfied with existing offerings?

CHAPTER 4   STRATEGY AND BUSINESS MODELS

There are certainly alternatives. A favorite of mine is to launch product (or service) offerings on a "platform" structure. This architecture allows adaptation of future features and technology to be integrated over the full life cycle of the core offering without major redesign. A classic example is the automobile where a variety of models can be integrated into a one frame platform.

- **Earnings per Share:** One of the classic measures of company performance is the relationship of earnings on a per share basis. It serves as an adequate indicator of an operation's overall performance but can mask weaknesses such a liquidity and other measures. In short, it begs the elements of shareholder value. Intuition alone isn't strong enough to assure validity of the information. This topic will be visited later in the text.

In his HBR article on "The True Measures of Success," the author, Michael Mauboussin (cited earlier), speaks to the issue of using intuitive measures. In his article he argues that they fall short of the connection between internal tasks and user applications. If this is true, then a more rigorous approach to measurements and the metrics we employ to capture true value creation should be undertaken. The complexity of valuation analytics may surpass these needs.

Execution

The assessment and execution of an organization's goals depend on the merging of multiple disciplines within an operation model. Failure to converge on agreed upon metrics usually reflects on one or more functional teams' lack of collaboration. The nexus of this usually resides on

CHAPTER 4   STRATEGY AND BUSINESS MODELS

the C level of the organization. They have both the viability and authority to deliver meaningfully to the valuation dialogue. In my discussions with 12 CEOs in preparation for this text, there was no consistent agreement to this assumption. They referenced examples lower in the organization. The term "garbage in, garbage out" was alluded to several times. This leaves us with at least two issues in the quest of overall valuation analytics: the first are agreed upon formulas of overall metrics; and the second the ability of the operating organization to supply the data needed for the assessment.

The paradox of this is that we have more sophisticated computational and analytical tools than we had previously. What is needed is concerted effort to focus and develop figures of merit of the overall entity. Conventional business models help forecast trends in the various functional areas of the organization. Tools to embrace comprehensive models of the organization as a whole seem to be lacking. The emerging disciplines of analytics offer promise but seem distant to the overall metrics needed.

Models

There are multiple models and avenues to pursue to achieve growth objectives. They lie in various functional areas of an organization. Some examples include

- Multiple distribution channels
- Alliances and joint ventures with other organizations
- Hiring personnel from new disciplines
- Licensing of IP toothers
- Seeking agreements from Global Partners

CHAPTER 4   STRATEGY AND BUSINESS MODELS

- Developing "families" of common technology products
- In-licensing of complementary products and technologies

When we look to cohesive models to rationalize potential growth opportunities, we find a lack of substantive choice. Experience suggests that the actual decision is subjective and lacks definitive analytical tools to help in decision-making. This uncertainty must be weighed against the risk of not reaching for new business opportunities.

Clayton Christensen, the Harvard Business School professor who argued for disruptive change in organizations, co-authored an article in *The Fall* 2016 issue of the *Sloan Management Review* entitled "The Hard Truth About Business Models." In the article, the authors deplore the lack of consistent models, yet they identify the elements of a business plan into three sections: they include the value of business priorities, the profit formula, and the resources to accomplish the goals.

Karan Girotra and Serguei Netessine, colleagues at INSEAD, write in their book *The Risk-Driven Business Model* (Harvard Business Press, 2014) about two types of risk in business plans. The first is "information risk" where decisions are made with insufficient information and the second is "incentive (mis)alignment risk" where the very individuals who contributed to the issues must execute the changes of the plan's proposal.

Allan Afuah, Professor of Business Strategy at the University of Michigan School of Business, writes about how technological innovation can be used to predict changes that can create value. His focus is on how companies such as Apple, Amazon, and Facebook have benefited from rapid change.

There seems to be a prevalent concern about the validity of business model and planning. It is clear that vibrant, healthy companies must constantly plan for future growth. Attention must be paid to the accuracy and detail in planning process.

CHAPTER 5

Organizational Impact and Corporate Culture

Of all the parts of a plan for growth that has impact on the commercial outcomes is the organizational model. How well the individual players (functions) interact to form a coherent outcome is the measure of the model's effectiveness. Someone once likened this to an orchestra whereas the different voices combine to a synergistic outcome. That may be a bit of a stretch, but the concept is valid.

A traditional model of authority and reporting has been jargoned as the "Rule of Six." In its simplest form, it says that there should only be six direct reports at any level of the organization. Graphically it looks like the model shown in Chapter 1.

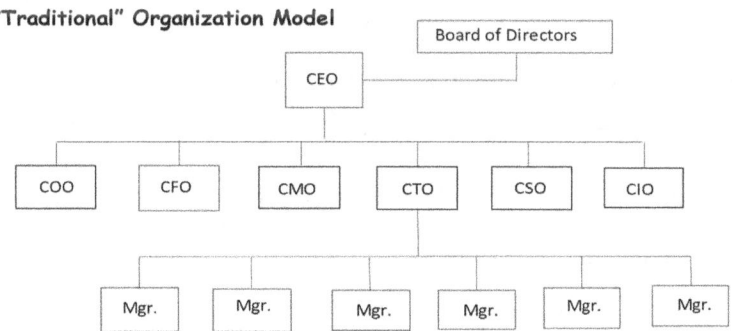

A hierarchal model such as this one allows for a clear definition of internal lines of communication and an opportunity to define channels of authority/decision-making. It is not the same for all business models. The actual working model matches the dynamics and demands of the selling cycle and industry standards.

There are certainly alternatives. A classic example is General Motors. In the United States, each product line has its own business unit called a division. There is a Chevrolet Division, a Buick Division, etc. Each has its own organizational hierarchy. It invites overlap as each division has its own CFO, CMO, etc. On the other hand, this model allows each division to adapt its organizational requirement and focus to its own needs.

Adaptive Organizations. Perhaps one of the most dynamic challenges facing an organization is that of adapting to and anticipating changes along the traditional growth curve. The organization that launches a new product or enterprise may not be the one that can create responses to the dynamics of growth. As products and organizations mature, the need for extending their life dynamics causes operating teams to invoke a different set of skills and experiences.

Within conventional organization, there are multiple means for providing the resources to assure that the dynamics are relevant to each segment of growth. Some of the more common tools include

- Continual in-house training and seminars
- Use of external consultants
- Sponsoring tuition for continuing education
- Use of 360 reviews and training
- Open "accounting" dialogue with upper management
- Offsite strategic meetings
- Reaching out to diversity and cultural perspective
- Organizational transition and stewardship

CHAPTER 5   ORGANIZATIONAL IMPACT AND CORPORATE CULTURE

This list is a "tip of the iceberg" for the organizational options available for projects and corporations in transition. Yet, the HR function seems somewhat buried in the corporate hierarchy. HR is certainly a significant cost center in the ongoing chart of accountants. The function is far from stage center in ongoing operations. New products, new markets, new financing, and even new technology easily command stage center in daily operations. If the impact of HR is so significant to ongoing outcomes, why is this possible?

There is an ongoing secrecy to many elements of the HR functions. Salaries, reviews (and their outcome changes), and even punitive actions are well within the realm of the HR-protected activities. This does not account for the rest of the list.

Attracting Talent. Perhaps one of the critical aspects of the HR function is the ability to attract and sustain the contributions of organizational talent. Nurturing talent is a critical element of this. This circles back to identifying an organization's medium- and long-term goals… and fitting the talent pool to meet them. Inherent in this is the need to nurture and improve these skills so no one is left behind. Perhaps one of the most discouraging exit interview declarations is an individual saying that they "didn't fit" in the organization and chose to leave. Beyond the personal angst, it's an expensive and discouraging position that reflects the shortfall of career planning in an organization. That juncture can be avoided with proper training support for an individual's career path within the context of longer-term goals.

Sources of Talent. The acquisition of talent is clearly an art form and requires all the finesse and skill of the "artists" that make it work. Some conventional sources include

- Executive recruiters (or "headhunters" as they are sometimes noted). Their specific contracts may be expensive, but they allow targeted campaigns. They tend to be used for senior positions.

- Advertisements in newspapers and journals. Generates responses but require sorting upon receipt. They are somewhat nondiscriminatory but offer outreach into specific populations.
- Internal bulletin boards and incentive plans for internal search capacity.
- Personal or professional contacts.

It is important to note that finding talent changes with the maturity of the organization. Attracting both hourly working and professional management changes with growth of a firm. The metamorphosis of skills and experiences required through journey on the "S" Curve changes in each phase. It becomes incumbent on management to provide pathways for change and support the individuals with both training and financial incentives. On a more sobering note, a percentage of all employees will not respond to these changes. Astute managers recognize this and act accordingly. Some individuals thrive at later stage issues and need to be brought in on a timely manner.

There are many sources beyond the abovementioned sample list. They seem to increase with the maturity of a given enterprise. There may be multiple organizational models to support early-stage growth. The Rule of Six model cited previously tends to support more mature growth. Early-stage entities are more fluid in their organizational model. Graphically, representations of organizations can be circular (see the following illustration) triangular, square, or whatever portrayal serves the operating teams best. What is most important is how well they serve to implement overall goals and mission objectives of the corporate entity. In addition, the operating models must serve as a two-way communication conduit for ongoing information flow. The organization must also serve to define authority and information feedback.

CHAPTER 5   ORGANIZATIONAL IMPACT AND CORPORATE CULTURE

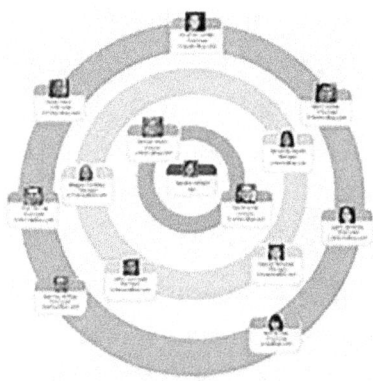

Larry Greiner, a professor at the University of Southern California (USC) Marshall School of Business, coined a representation of the phases of organizational growth called the Greiner Curve (see the following illustration). He identified six stages of the process. They include the following:

- **Growth Through Creativity**: Characterized by individuals wearing many hats. Communication is both spontaneous and informal. Certain industries move through this phase faster than others. For example, a high-growth technology organization will move faster than a structured financial institution.

- **Growth Through Direction**: The early stage of leadership. Functional roles are forming and specialty skills in new market and technology offerings must also emerge. Early indicators of project scale exceeding the ability of individual contributors.

- **Growth Through Delegation**: Layers of hierarchy appear. Top management becomes less involved in day-to-day operations. The need for standardized procedures appears. The role of contributors lends weight to increased communications skills and increased emphasis on teamwork.

CHAPTER 5   ORGANIZATIONAL IMPACT AND CORPORATE CULTURE

- **Growth Through Coordination**: New policies and procedures are introduced with the goal of improved collaboration and utilization of resources. The risk of additional "red tape" being absorbed increases. It is a formula for crisis of efficiency and allocation of resources.

- **Growth Through Collaboration**: At this stage of growth, an organization moves from bureaucratic systems to the give-and-take of collaboration. New internal skills are required, and new communication tools must be embraced. Development of collaboration models becomes essential for integration of outside opportunities.

- **Growth Through Alliances**: The door of opportunity opens to a new means of operation. Partnering with other organizations, outsourcing (including licensing), mergers, and acquisitions now enter the corporate vocabulary. This creates the need for corporate models to revisit the vision and mission of the organization because it no longer relies on internal strengths.

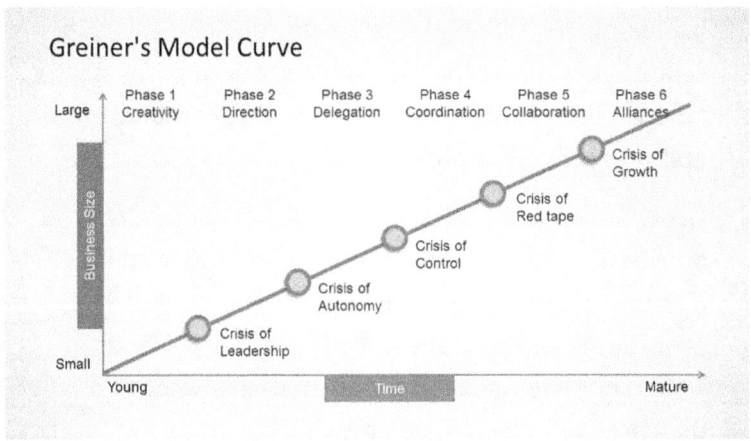

Greiner Curve is replicated in many venues. In fact, it is one of many attempts to capture the dynamics of change on the internal organizational model. One message permeates the story. It is the importance of looking ahead and anticipating the changes. The need for changes is significant throughout the journey of the "S" Curve. Leadership resides in the anticipation of changes and the nimble, proactive responses to both internal and external challenges.

CHAPTER 6

Resource Acquisition

In the planning for a flight in an airplane, meticulous attention is focused on the calculation of the required amount of fuel essential for a successful journey. Yet, even with allowances for reserves, fuel starvation accidents are still reported. Maybe it may not be as dramatic as aircraft fuel starvation, but the improper calculation of human, technical, and financial resources required for a successful venture carries an analogous sense of failure through starvation. Let us look at the various components in more detail:

- **Capital and Financial Considerations**: When marketing and engineering organizational resources are diminished to an unusable level, there are usually remedies available. They may be rented, shared, and procured even with unreasonable terms. This is not so for financial capital. When an organization depletes its capital (or cash), it indicates a failure of the project. It is likened to an airplane flying a course becoming depleted of fuel. In flying, it is called fuel starvation.

    The conditions that accompany cash infusions at this point of the journey usually carry with them unfavorable terms:

CHAPTER 6   RESOURCE ACQUISITION

- Loans may carry rigid repayment terms and higher than normal fees and interest rates. The quality of the lending source will certainly no be the A team. That, in turn, affects further borrowing capacity.

- Equity infusions at times of crisis are not usually considered an option. Lopsided valuations and excessive terms and conditions can appear and even the governance models in the company may be altered in the sense that additional board seats may accrue to the new investors.

- Non-dilutive cash in the form of government contracts, grants, and even gifts (scholarships) are always possible. Most take significant time/effort to process and are complicated in their support paperwork. They usually incur extensive reporting efforts.

- Trade considerations are time worn sources of capital. Down payments, discounts, and progress payments are in the same category. They are important to nurture in less than critical times. Unfortunately, they do not enter the dialogue enough. An alert Board might challenge upper management to considering these on a regular basis.

Whatever dreadful scenario confronts a company at the end of capital/cash, these events are avoidable. Are the CEO/treasurer functions attuned to cash conservation, and are documents such as the monthly statement of cash flows being utilized?

In addition to tactical concerns, we should ask if the governance function (including the Board of Directors) both participate and demand accountability. They play a crucial role in the positive outcomes. The price of governance function indifference is significant.

Accounting Tools (the Balance Sheet): Of all the financial tools that are available, the Balance Sheet remains all powerful. It literally deals with the financial strength of the organization (Assets) and obligations against them (Liabilities). It is typically reported monthly. The structure of a Balance Sheet is well known. We deal with its contents each month in our personal lives. We look at the various bills and obligations we have as individuals (Liabilities?) and compare them to the resources of monies and credits we must use to support them (Assets?). The accounting perspective adds both structure and depth to the discussion. In addition, it delineates the financial aspects of the owner's participation as a category of Liabilities. The familiar equation of the Balance Sheet is shown as

$$\text{Assets} + \text{Liabilities and Owner's Equity}$$

In graphic form:

PREMIER TOOLS AND CONSOLIDATED SUBSIDIARY Balance Sheet March 31, 20X3						
Assets			**Liabilities**			
Current assets			Current liabilities			
Cash	$150,000		Accounts payable	$160,000		
Trading securities	70,000		Salaries payable	30,000		
Accounts receivable	110,000		Interest payable	10,000	$200,000	
Inventories	220,000	$550,000				
			Long-term liabilities			
Property, plant & equipment			Notes payable	$240,000		
Land	$135,000		Mortgage liability	110,000	350,000	
Buildings and equipment (net)	375,000	510,000			$550,000	
Intangible assets			**Stockholders' equity**			
Patent	$225,000		Capital stock	$300,000		
Goodwill	65,000	290,000	Retained earnings	500,000	800,000	
Total assets		$1,350,000	**Total liabilities and equity**		$1,350,000	

Figure 6-1. *Balance Sheet Format*

CHAPTER 6 RESOURCE ACQUISITION

A first observation is that things we own (Assets) are delineated on the left side of the sheet. It does not matter if it is the Balance Sheet of a startup or a Fortune 500 entity. The format is the same. The items are presented in descending order of their liquidity. They are further grouped into short- and long-term items. Items such as Cash are shown first as they can be converted (Liquidity) quickly. Inventory comes next. Although not quite as nimble or liquid, unused Inventory can be converted to cash. Accounts Receivable follow. These obligations can be factored and converted to cash, albeit in a more complicated and time-consuming process.

As the list continues, we move into buildings (real estate), machinery, and softer items such as intellectual property and goodwill. The summation of it all is a rendering of the Total Assets of the company.

On the right side of the document are the charges to these Assets. Stating a large cash amount but carrying significant loans against that amount opens a first clue as to how the Balance Sheet presents a picture of the company. Let us look at the individual items. Like Assets, they are presented in descending order of liquidity. One of the top items is Accounts Payable. Although constrained by legal obligations, they are variable in the sense of when the items will be paid. Of course, it is not open-ended and is limited by items such as available cash and external credit ratings.

As the items accrue on the Balance Sheet in terms of increasing non-liquidity, a notation on long-term Liabilities such as real estate mortgages appears. A real estate or equipment lease might have a term of 30 years. The impact of this is to cause a constant monthly drain on the available cash and thus impair decisions about nimble acquisitions of other strategies for growth. They are not simple entries.

A third category of entries on the Liability side of the Balance Sheet is called Shareholder's Equity. It is a delineation of the shareholder's equity participation. To present it in financial terms, a "par" estimate value is attached to each share. Upon liquidation, the actual selling price is computed to the individual shares. The final category of entries on the

Balance Sheet is the cumulative Profit and Loss entries of Net Income/Loss that are derived from the income statement. They are referred to as retained earnings. In a sense these entries are owed to the owners of the company.

Ratios (the Dynamic Comparator): Various observers of Balance Sheet entries look for different aspects of an entity's performance. Investors and banking professionals are interested in the utilization of financial resources and certainly their effective use. Internal managers might be interested in the operating efficiency of the operations. Both interests can be satisfied by certain ratios. In addition, those numbers can offer a window to the relative performance to industry standards and certainly competitive analysis.

An example of this is the ratio of Assets to Liabilities. It is called the Current Ratio. Clearly stated, it is

$$Current\ Ratio = Assets/Liabilities$$

This number reveals how well incoming Assets such as Accounts Receivable generated from Sales is matched to the drain of loans and Accounts Payable. More importantly does this number reveal how much reserve a company has for new investments ranging from technology development to acquisitions. A number of 2.0 is considered healthy but somewhat dependent on its trend from previous accountings and industry comparables to find a perspective. Implications range from strategies to acquisitions to more efficient use of cash for inventory turn improvements or new equipment purchases.

Not all ratios deal with external measures of performance. Inventory turnover, for example, is a measure of the efficiency of cash utilization gleaned from how often the inventory is utilized. In computation terms, it is simply stated

$$Inventory\ Turnover = Cost\ of\ Goods\ Sold/Average\ Inventory$$

CHAPTER 6   RESOURCE ACQUISITION

This is important because it deals with cash utilization. As stated before, good cash management allows for many forward transactions ranging from internal investment to external "M and A" activity. To some, inventory management may not be as exciting as other operational activities, but cash utilization certainly is.

There are about a dozen ratios that can be used to characterize a company's financial performance. They are stated in most accounting handbooks. Their importance is that they allow trend comparison and industry comparable analysis to investors and other outside sources. They also allow internal comparisons to other investments in their portfolios. In common, they are not absolute measures but allow comparative analysis.

Financial Markets: Till now, we have looked at sources of cash in a somewhat neutral manner. Sources of cash vary. Each has different characteristics and varies on their impact on the organization.

- The broad categories include:
  - Cash generated from internal operations
  - Informal sources such as personal funds and FFF
  - Early-stage Angel investors
  - Venture capital investors
  - Investment banking
  - External "M and A" transactions
  - Internal Operations-Generated Cash
    - When revenue from operations exceeds both fixed and variable expenditures, certainly profits can be generated. In addition, cash is accumulated in this transaction. Thus, daily sales transactions become a source of cash.

CHAPTER 6   RESOURCE ACQUISITION

There may be variability in this as discounts and special offers created to induce sales can limit the amount of free cash available.

- The issues occur when the sources of generated capital do not meet the requirements of growth. Also, large capital investments such as property acquisitions or plant and equipment demands are larger than the available capital generations capacity. Certainly, mortgages and loans can mitigate the impact of these excursions, but their management is different than the requirements of working capital. Nor is it clear that the skills and experiences of the management team are in place for this shift. All this must be evaluated before the transactions occur… and supportive corrections are in place.

- **Informal and Non-dilutive Sources of Capital Acquisition**
    - In the spectrum of corporate entities, there are various levels of capital acquisition formality. At one end, there are proprietorships and family-run models that have available sources such as family and friends (remember FFF) and self-funding. At the other end, there are sophisticated debt funding schemes available. In common, they tend to be non-equity which preserves the stock dilution of equity financing. However, they carry the responsibility of repayment (with interest). In interviews with early-stage executives, this was expressed as a

57

prejudice against short-term loans. The penalty of nonpayment threatens the very liquidity of the entity. In the realm of larger, more structured instruments, collateral in terms of equipment liens or real estate holding mitigates some of the risks.

- **Early-Stage Angel Investors**
  - About 40 years ago, a professor at the University of New Hampshire named Bill Wetzel observed the behavior of a group of retired Route 128 (the technology highway that circles Boston) executives that had "cashed" out from their technology- based companies and had moved to New Hampshire to retire (sort of). However, they were not just playing golf or fishing. Rather they were making investments in early- stage ventures. Not only were they using their own capital, but they offered contacts and experience in their respective fields. Professor Wetzel likened them to the investors that funded Broadway shows and were called Angels – the term struck. What was to change is that their investments moved from individual investor deals to those made by Bands of Angels as they were called. This was later morphed into a "national" trade organization called the Angel Capital Association (ACA).

CHAPTER 6   RESOURCE ACQUISITION

Although an enticing and accessible source of capital and experience for early-stage projects, they lacked the "deep pockets" required to fund subsequent rounds needed for the long-term growth of the companies. Formal venture capital was required for that.

- **The Formality of Venture Capital**
  - In 1946 a group of individuals based in Boston recognized a need for a more systematic source of early-stage capital for new technology-based ventures. A leader of this initiative was Georges Doriot. The concept of utilizing outside investments from "limited partners" and subjecting those investments to professional investors was not entirely new... but the focus of those deals on technology-based firms was.

    Doriot and his partners called the investment firm American Research and Development Corporation (ARDC) and located it in Boston. Their portfolio targeted technology-based companies. Being located "across the river" from MIT was not an accident. In addition to the proximity as an asset, the firm realized that many soldiers were returning from World War 2 and were eager to utilize their experiences and newly minted credentials in entrepreneurial startups. The legacy spilled over to Doriot himself. He was dubbed the "father of modern venture capital."

CHAPTER 6   RESOURCE ACQUISITION

One investment made in the early days of ARDC has become legion. It involved a new company in Maynard, MA, called Digital Equipment Corporation (DEC). It was founded by an MIT escapee named Ken Olsen. DEC pioneered the development and application of midsized computers. Until that time computers built by IBM, Sperry, and others were room-sized machines. The DEC machines were smaller, lighter, and faster than the historical predecessors. The amount of the AR and investment was $70,000. It also carried about $200,000 in debt. When liquidated, the investment was valued at hundreds of millions. It became a bellwether for venture capital deals.

The term venture capital had its origins in a report issued in 1920 by the American Bankers Association where forms of speculative investing were acknowledged and deemed "good for the development and growth" of the country. The focus on technology-based companies that were the mantra of ARDC became the basis for the term as used today.

- **Timing:** Where an organization on the life cycle curve affects which sources of capital are available to them. Pictorially, this is shown in the following.

CHAPTER 6   RESOURCE ACQUISITION

Commercialization Cycle...

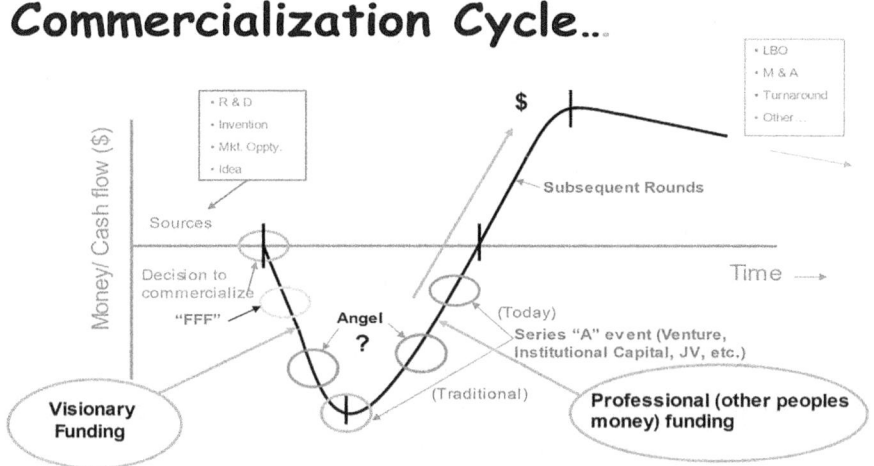

In the early stages, a project is not a good candidate for bank loans or investment capital. There is simply not enough data or collateral to support those transactions. Bank loans require collateral by both federal rules and local bylaws. Certain transactions such as real estate or capital equipment have the substance to support that type of effort.

The capital needed to support growth must come from subsequent rounds of risk or venture capital. In the venture world, these rounds are delineated by the term series with alphabetical identifiers (i.e., "Series A"). Each round is supported by a document called terms and conditions that explain how subsequent rounds are structured to protect the percentage equity interests of the earlier rounds.

CHAPTER 6 RESOURCE ACQUISITION

There are non-dilutive mechanisms for investments such as government (SBIR) and foundation grants that do not require equity to support them. They are attractive but usually do not have the scope to support strong growth initiatives.

- **Needs:** In the earlier discussions, it was pointed out in a break-even model that each unit sold after fixed and variable costs are supported yields positive contributions to earnings. But the investment demands of people and organizational infrastructure, technology, plant, and equipment exceed that earning capacity... and set up the need for external infusion of capital.

- **Beyond Early-Stage Capital:** When the resources and capital of early-stage capital are exploited, more substantive sources appear that can provide not only more financial resources of more magnitude but also open the options of joint ventures, mergers, and limited partnerships. The creativity of investment bankers and equity partners that guide those deals usually come from the investment banking industry and carry a different mindset than the earlier venture capitalists that were so important to the earlier chapters.

With this comes the requirement that the internal teams must become more sophisticated and experienced. The formality of the chief financial officer (CFO) becomes in focus at an accelerating pace. Other members of the "C" level of management must also mature. It is not uncommon for various team members to attend seminars and short courses to enhance their ability to manage later-stage challenges.

Forms of Investment. Although capital formation is focused on the acquisition of cash, there are multiple forms of investment available. Cash, of course, is critical. It solves the lag between income and expense (working capital) and allows acquisition of both plant equipment and production capacity. Some of this is circular. A piece of automation equipment (robots) can improve productivity and the resultant profitability. Machinery and building capacity become essential for growth of an entity.

There are alternatives. Accounts Receivable, for example, can be "factored" against loan instruments. Another example are the mortgages and long-term debt instruments that allow for more substantive investments. One addition that is clearly available to managers is lean manufacturing. Productivity gains and improving inventory "turns" are just examples. These terms apply to both hard goods and service-based operations.

Other Forms of Acquisition. With growth and more substantial Balance Sheet composition comes an array of additional alternatives. For example, merging (or forming joint ventures) with a company that has a cash-rich Balance Sheet but lacks technology or market presence (or both) might be a logical next step. In today's global economies, a partnership with companies in both the cultures and markets seems to be quite logical. One only has to survey the business trade papers to see verification of this.

CHAPTER 7

Allocation of Resources

The search for and the acquisition of capital and other resources is considered glamorous by some. Of interest now is how are these resources utilized and how the supporting decisions to utilize them are made. Finally, it becomes of interest to measure the outcomes of the use of these resources. Did they accomplish the desired result?

The Impetus. The focus of an organization to grow has its roots in the very bedrock of the vision, goals, and the objectives of the project. This applies to individual projects as well as to corporate entities. Growth is not an illusionary issue, rather it is a concrete set of directions of effort and resources. It is extended to many levels by applied budgets, plans, and actual tasks. The dialogue starts in exchanges between corporate governance and Board of Directors. The Boards are the custodians of the shareholder interests. The management represents the company, the people, the technology, and the ability to execute on them.

Vision. Much has been written about the creation and execution of a central vision and setting of future goals. Clarity of vision allows accurate forecasting, manpower planning, clarity of long-range capital expenditures, etc. How that vision is communicated to the organization

CHAPTER 7   ALLOCATION OF RESOURCES

and how it is inculcated to ongoing decision-making are a bit of mystery. There are essentially three strategies:

- The first is a "top-down" approach. In this scenario, a form of edict document is issued from top management and left to be assimilated by the organization. Little dialogue (or "buy in") results from this approach. In larger organizations, this model may make sense.

- The second is a "bottom-up" approach where dialogue starts at the working level of the organization and works its way up to the operating management of the organization. "Buy in" is quite effective and the resultant engagement is more productive. A stellar example of this is Ben and Jerry's located in Waterbury, Vermont. In a public corporate document's Q and A section, they describe factory tours available to the public. Renditions of the corporate vision are secured in many places during the walking part of the tour to offer to visitors. In taking such a tour, the guide suggests that the implementation of the vision to each working level of the organization is an important company value. Visitors are encouraged to interrogate any worker to test this concept. I encountered a maintenance person on one of the tours and asked him to articulate the company statement and cite an example of its application. He did so flawlessly. It can be done.

- The third option is to allow the issue to float through the organization and not give it much credence. This certainly will produce predicable outcomes. Unfortunately, this option is more common than it should be.

CHAPTER 7   ALLOCATION OF RESOURCES

Empowering Leadership. Beyond the issues outlined earlier about the strategy of driving the vision statement into the organization, there is a larger matter of integrating the elements of the vision into the organization and empowering the organization's structure to act on it to produce measurable results:

- The starting point is to look at the governance model. The Board of Directors and the upper C-level management play a crucial role in this. This is accomplished by constant dialogue with other elements of the organization and participating in ongoing decision behavior. Those individuals must "walk the talk" of the implementation. In my role as senior executive of my company, I was constantly judged by what I did... as well as what I said. This process is not without issues. Perhaps a primary one was communication. I encouraged monthly employee sessions about implementation issues. Of importance was that a two-way dialogue ensued. Learning to listen effectively was invaluable.

- The organizational environment sets the stage for this shift of the vision to the inner workings from upper management. There are endless models of the organization that are suited to the business needs of the business. A classic one is based on the IBM Rule of Six. It is simply an organizational construct that limits the number of direct reports to six (see Figure 1-3). It applies to all levels of the organization. It was a standard approach to organizational structure. With the external pressures of innovation, global commerce, and new means of funding, the models now are judged on being nimble, adaptive, disruptive, and other metrics that weren't considered central when the original hierarchal models were in vogue. It forces the discussion to be adaptive to the implications of growth.

- Leadership in a growing organization is a dynamic and changing landscape. It is of importance that issues of constant improvement and nimble adaptation are under constant review.

Critical Resources. What are the resources that should be considered? Certainly not all of them are equally important at the same time. Some common examples include:

- **Human:** Certainly, a critical resource for any emerging company. The skills and professional experiences that are required in the early stages must constantly be nurtured along a company's path to growth. New incentive plans, increased incentive programs, latest software tools for support, and improved recruiting are all part of the new tools for companies' maturity.

- **Financial:** Clearly a most important element for allocation of resources. The scope and formality of financial resources increase with the maturity of the organization. The CFO and treasurer functions play increasingly important roles in the journey toward growth. Internally, budgets become more formal as do internal controls. Perhaps the most important change occurs in the planning of future needs. Relatively small and flexible arrangements can be accomplished in early-stage enterprises. This is not the case as the organizations mature and progress up the growth ("S" Curves).

- **Plant and Equipment/Automation:** Certain decisions require long-term application and planning process times. Examples include buildings, equipment, automation and information systems, and global IP protection. With long-term payoffs, some of these decisions require mortgages and long-term leases as well as individuals to program and manage them. None of these are critical but require new management disciplines in long-term decision dynamics. Certainly, they can be anticipated… but need care in the differences in application dynamics.

Larger Balance Sheet Issues. There are a series of transactions that occur at the corporate Balance Sheet level. They fall into the categories of mergers and acquisitions (M & A), joint ventures, technology licensing, etc. In common, they involve corporate-level decisions and even may include equity (stock) as part of the consideration. They tend to occur later in the "S" Curve life cycle because of their substance. In addition, they are substantive enough to involve the Board of Directors and other elements of the governance model.

CHAPTER 8

Market and Branding Considerations

Marketing is a unique discipline. It does not stand alone in an organization. In its basic definition, marketing has the responsibility to establish the value of the entity's offering. The marketing function is clearly differentiated from the selling effort. It is integrated with customer influences, external demographics, external competitive pressures, internal (and external) needs for brand identity, sales force support, and others. Yet, it typically commandeers single-digit percentage allocation of sales revenue. Marketing provides a critical link between the corporate vision and the customer. Although a separate function, the sales effort is to provide closure to the customer's purchasing decision process.

Framework

Professor Benson Shapiro, from the Harvard Business School, wrote a text entitled "The Marketing Process" (HBS No. 584-146, 1984) where he explained that marketing is a six-part process, which includes

1. **Marketing Strategy Formation**: Set the overall long-term goals and basic approach to the marketplace. This typically involves making choices about specific customer groups to serve, customer needs to address, and the best way to create value for the customer.

2. **Marketing Planning**: Depending on the industry, the time horizon for planning can vary. In dynamic situations, for example, in a technology-driven industry, plans need to be reworked regularly. In slower, more stable situations, the basics of planning might extend over two to three years.

3. **Programming, Allocating, and Budgeting**: Set near-term objectives and detailed plans (typically once a year), including how resources will be allocated to the necessary activities.

4. **Implementation**: Execute the programs specified in step 3.

5. **Monitoring and Auditing**: Evaluate results against goals and develop corrective plans as needed.

6. **Analysis and Research**: Gather necessary data from inside and outside the company to support the first four action steps. This data gathering should occur before executing each of the four steps and should be ongoing.

Possibly one of the prominent aspects of the marketing function is to identify competitive influences and to develop strategies for confronting them. Peter Drucker, in *Management Challenges for the 21st Century* (HarperCollins, 1999), cited that marketing and innovation are the two driving forces for successful growth. It became an important theme in his professional work.

Dick Morley, renowned engineer and innovator, collaborated with Ralph Grabowski, marketing consultant, in a paper entitled "The Voice of Dick Morley and Ralph Grabowski." It was edited by Thomas Smeenk, CEO of Hemostemix (April 2020). The theme of the article was that the number of resources allocated to marketing and engineering should at least be 1:1 in favor of marketing. Grabowski later argued the ratio should be at

CHAPTER 8   MARKET AND BRANDING CONSIDERATIONS

least 2:1. In both cases, the article favored a predominance of marketing allocations over engineering.

Marketing. The function of marketing has many dimensions. Some aspects rely on the industry/market segment in which they choose to do business. External influences include government regulations. These influences can be quite pervasive and can reach down into the very product offerings. Examples lie in medical products and services, food and safety equipment offering, and larger industries like aviation. Beyond government intervention, there is trade protocol. An example is the Microsoft Windows 10 Operating Systems. Were a company to elect to write software and even the many apps now in vogue, it must observe the Windows protocol and nuances in their development... wow!

Still, there are significant areas assigned to the marketing function. Some aspects (not in order) include

- Demographic delineation:
    - Who are the customers?
    - Where do they reside?
    - Economic and family particulars.
- Competitive influences
- Pricing (and discounts)
- Feature/benefit definition
- Promotion
- Trade show visibility
- Advertising
- Packaging
- Distribution scenarios
- Warranty and support

CHAPTER 8   MARKET AND BRANDING CONSIDERATIONS

What is so intriguing is the scope of marketing outreach. Its integration to technology development, finance, internal operations, and the overall value proposition of the entity are huge. The articulation of this function is a critical tab of the business plan notebook. Of interest is that many marketing expenditures occur before the product is even released and sold. This makes it an investment as well as an ongoing expenditure. The results of successful marketing investments contribute significantly to the overall value proposition of the company.

CHAPTER 9

Capital/Financial Considerations

Corporate growth is clearly a confluence of multiple factors that must collaborate on a shared vision for the enterprise. One element deserves more attention than the others. It is the acquisition of and allocation of capital. It stands alone in that no function can contribute to the overall vision without sustaining capital. How are the decisions to allow investment in each company or project made? What are the investor criteria? Without this knowledge, a scenario for failure ensues. Let us look at the elements. A tool that helps visualize this is the "S" Curve or life cycle graphic.

The elements fall into three broad categories in the life cycle of a project or company.

CHAPTER 9   CAPITAL/FINANCIAL CONSIDERATIONS

Commercialization Cycle...

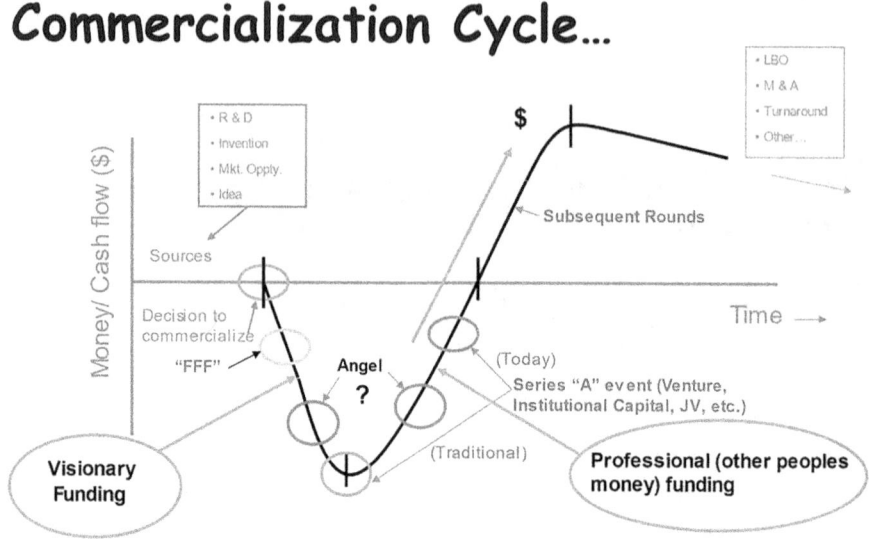

Figure 9-1. The Funding Cycle

- The first category is envisioned as the **startup phase**. Since there is little offsetting revenue at this point in an organization's journey, outside sources must be utilized. There are multiple possibilities:

    - Non-dilutive agencies such as Small Business Innovation Research (SBIR)grants. Others in this category include the National Science Foundation (NSF). Defense Department grants under Defense Advanced Research Projects Agency (DARPA). This list can be extended to many government/ philanthropic organizations such as the Ford Foundation and many others in this category. In common, they are non-equity dilutive. They tend

CHAPTER 9   CAPITAL/FINANCIAL CONSIDERATIONS

to have significant reporting and public exposure requirements. A classic example of this form of funding is that the Internet we started by DARPA contracts... wow.

- The next step in the early-stage funding journey is referred to as friends, family, and fools (FFF). As its name implies, it is a source of capital that is driven by motives other than return on investment (ROI). It is usually driven by and belief in the entrepreneur and their ideas. The "fool" aspect is that it is so early in the life cycle that there is little information to support the decision process. It is driven by ideas, not substantive analysis. Also, the documentation that tends to support these investments is light and can prove to be problematic in later, more formal stages.

- A next step in this journey is to look at equity-based investments. The area is generally referred to as Angel investment. Angels is a term created by Professor William (Bill) Wetzel about 30 years ago. Bill was at the University of New Hampshire in Durham, NH. He observed that there was a group of investors who had in common that they had "cashed out" from their technology-based companies and had enough personal liquidity to invest in early-stage, Boston-based companies. Bill coined them Angel investors because their behavior was likened to the group of early-stage Broadway investors (Angels) who invested in early-stage theater offerings in similar circumstances. They were individuals who not only invested their own capital but also offered the experience and know-how to the projects in which they invested.

CHAPTER 9   CAPITAL/FINANCIAL CONSIDERATIONS

Even though there was a highly individualistic aspect to early Angel investing, several changes occurred that altered the landscape. As individual Angel investors, the amount or investment capability is limited. This is offset by the professional expertise and perspective they offer. Today, Angel investing has increased its professionalism and even tout a national organization of best practices called the Angel Capital Association.

Beyond Angel investing, there is a place for non-dilutive investment. It takes the form of grants and non-stock investments. Even down payments on future product or service deliveries fall into this category.

- The threshold for venture capital is somewhat more rigorous. This is understandable as "other peoples' money" is involved. Also, the amount of investment is larger than what is typically offered by Angel investments and grants. These limitations are mitigated by a new breed of venture investing coined "early-stage" venture investing. This source emerged because of the need for funding of a relatively new breed of ventures.

- Limited partners in the venture capital firms that work in this area expect large return (20x) and are alert to the area of risk and failure along the way. The risk/reward aspects are known and anticipated. The emergence of Angel (individual) investors who bring an additional dimension of industry perspective and experience to the process helps shift the ratio to more positive outcome. In the term sheets that accompany these early investments, there are both antidilution provisions and investment linkages for subsequent rounds. These first rounds are called Series A events.

- The second stage is one of **growth**. A different mindset accompanies this round of investments. Since the sales offerings have proven their customer viability in the early stage, the attention now shifts to the sustainable nature of the offering. Exposition of a sales engine to continue growth and the allocation of resources to drive the momentum are now in focus. Externally, competitive pressures, regulatory and trade issues, and, of course, brand identity become the subject of discussion.

- The third stage is one of **maturity**. Although this suggests the end of original life cycle, it offers multiple opportunities and platforms for new growth. Some possibilities include product extensions, market variations, and product options. The concept of platforms for a "family of products" becomes enticing. Beyond this there are other paths including corporate mergers, joint ventures, and licensing to extend the potential of the original efforts.

No matter which stage of maturity an investment project is, there are certain identifiable metrics that are used to characterize the investment. They are mostly financial but also include references to performance and industry comparables.

CHAPTER 9 CAPITAL/FINANCIAL CONSIDERATIONS

The basic questions that acquiring financial resources raises are, at minimum, fundamental. Examples include the following:

- What tangible return will be received from the required investment? This concept is referred to as return on investment (ROI). Each investment source has its own criteria for ROI over a given period. The investment project must envision an equal or larger forecast for its returns. There are exceptions of course. For example, an investment might be considered for strategic reasons such as entry into new market or technology while falling short of financial objectives. These are considered exceptions because an investment company's goals are centered on numerical returns to the limited partners (or investors) to which the firm (or fund) is accountable.

- Further strategic considerations include making multiple investments in a given market or technology. This process "hedges the bet" to assure that the winnings in a given sector are realized. This option applies to new or evolving opportunities. It also embraces the model of "portfolio management" which helps define a given funds identity.

- Beyond financial metrics, there are a series of significant "other" measures. For example, if the stated vision of an enterprise is to become a dominant player in a given field, then the issues and measures of market share become stage center. Other supporting metrics such as inventory turns may be viewed with less importance. This again supports the sense that clearly articulated (and communicated) visions become essential to sustainable growth models.

- What is an interesting artifact of this process is the lack of ongoing attention it receives on a normal basis. Should not it be part of the governance agenda? Valuation metrics, although challenging in its mathematical derivations, is a valuable guidepost. Typically, these calculations engaged at startup financing and liquidation transactions. It seems it ought to be monitored as a regular metric.

Process. Much attention has been focused on the value of allocation of resources in the management of enterprises. How does it work, and what might be best practices? A starting point is to look at a conventional "bottom-up" process.

- **Sources of Data**: Multiple sources of information are gleaned for the operating arms of an organization. Sales projections, market assessments, and technology forecasts generated by those individuals who have direct responsibility to them should have the most relevant data available. This data gathering requires judgment to manage. In my company, for example, we used a model of a sale's "funnel" (see Figure 9-2). It required a knowledge of the sales process and how potential customer decisions affecting orders occur. Over time the predictive accuracy of the model increased to a level that allowed us a 5% accuracy of a year's forecast. Since the sales cycle was a long one, this allowed the materials planning organization to be quite accurate in their procurement functions.

CHAPTER 9   CAPITAL/FINANCIAL CONSIDERATIONS

Figure 9-2. *The Sales Funnel*

Consolidation of Data. The next step in this process is to consolidate (and integrate) the various proposals. This is usually managed by the chief financial officer (CFO) or their designees. It is not an easy task. If done well, it reveals conflicting and competing goals and expectations beyond the financial capacity of the company. A more formidable situation occurs when the budgetary expectations are below the capacity. That situation speaks to a culture that lacks both imagination and creativity. Robert Browning, the renowned poet, said that "a man's reach should exceed his grasp, or what's a heaven for?"

- With the consolidation and conflict issues resolved, the process moves to top management and the governance process for approval. It could be the arena for further debate; the set of conflicts can be ameliorated by setting the goals and vision with clarity. At best a healthy dialogue of objective can be accomplished. Operationally, both internal and external conditions change. Budget processes need to provide contingency funds and reserves as an element of the process.

CHAPTER 9   CAPITAL/FINANCIAL CONSIDERATIONS

- An important phase of the process is the communication of the consolidated budget to the organization so operational decisions and projects can be secured. An essential part of this task is to establish metrics for how well the allocation elements are being accomplished with respect to the budgetary goals. It needs to be monitored continuously as there is no way the corrections can be accomplished at the end of the allocated time periods.

- There is a somewhat onerous and detailed document that accompanies an investment. It is called terms and conditions. It asserts the control and boundaries of the investment source and company to which it is made. It is as powerful as the ability to hire/fire the CEO and management. It delineates participation of the Board of Directors and its member composition. The more positive side of this document defines the basis for subsequent rounds of investment such that it allows for an orderly dilution of ownership. Without this, it would be close to impossible to attract new sources into a growing entity.

CHAPTER 10

The Role of Technology

Technology is a broad term. It embraces product designs, marketing features, performance/benefit arguments, and certainly brand identity (i.e., Intel Inside). It also impacts the allocation of resources to maintain leadership in each field. Technology has two major areas of impact to the success of a project: the first deals with the actual product or service offerings; and the second deals with the internal workings of the operation. Let us look at both.

There has been an astonishing rate of movement to drive computation and information processing to lower levels. The supporting design of apps and software has enabled this. Automobiles are good examples of this. There are as many as 17 separate processors on the modern car. Seats, radios, lights, and heaters each have their own processing circuits. Each one is smaller and more embedded than its predecessor. The result of this is the evolution of "smart" devices. In addition, the cost per bit has dropped exponentially. A computer that might have cost over $1,000 a few years ago is now in the low hundreds. On the one hand, this extends the reach of the computational contribution while it also commoditizes its value. The rush to larger-scale integration of information and faster processing speeds adds additional burden to the cost. The process relies on broader market penetration to distribute development costs.

CHAPTER 10   THE ROLE OF TECHNOLOGY

Gordon Moore, one of the founders of the Intel Corporation, commented on this trend by predicting that processing circuits would double in their computational capacity in each generation's release. The idea was coined Moore's Law. It is still not clear what the impact of this dynamic on the commercial value is on this computational capacity. Innovation will increasingly rely on the applications of the technology – not the technology itself.

"S" Commercialization Cycles...

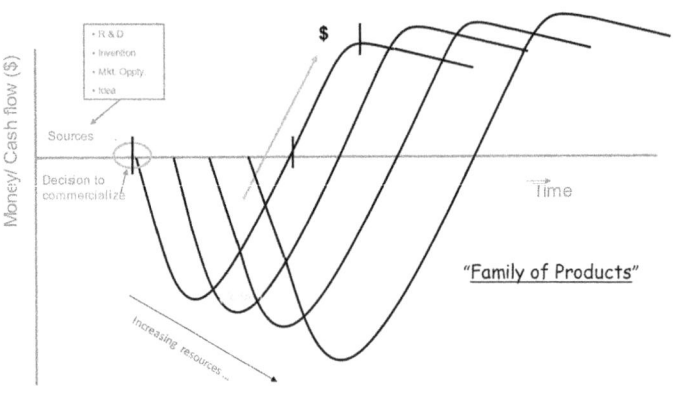

One solution is to envision "families" of products and applications that are based on one technology platform. One enabling technology could be used for multiple applications and even multiple markets. Clarity of long-term goals helps this process as the platforms can be designed to be robust enough to sustain multiple applications.

Certain enabling technologies allow multiple life cycles to be built into the base architecture. An example is the microprocessor computational chip. It is expensive to design and produce but easy to allow multiple iterations of a platform of uses to be designed at one time. Just changing the programing or pin location could allow access to multiple functionalities. As this is certainly easier and cost-effective than creating a

CHAPTER 10   THE ROLE OF TECHNOLOGY

new platform for each use, in addition, the development and tooling costs are amortized over several application families.

There is an analogy to mechanical components used in a potential family of products. Processes such as forging and casting are quite expensive and require significant time to execute. If space or design features can be allocated to allow a similar "family" of designs that were cited previously, the effort can be utilized throughout the product design cycle. Reductions in design time and costs can also be allocated over several iterations of the product life cycle. Reductions in time to market are also available in this approach.

There is an art form to managing multiple life cycles. It lies in the realm of marketing. The very operating system that this text is controlled by Microsoft design. It is about to release its eleventh iteration. Yet, I can move through documents written in all the earlier levels of the operating releases. Although Microsoft does not "support" the earlier versions anymore, they are still quite accessible and supported by independent sources. There is a large enough installed base to financially support this.

The lure of operational efficiency and new features is enough to encourage the acquisition of the next generations. The thought that earlier versions will someday lack support is a subtle additional inducement.

Protection

Since research and development is a significant investment of revenue dollars (between 10% and 15%), there arises a need to protect the "value" of those investments. The Federal government and various international agencies provide this in the form of intellectual protection (patents and copyrights). It is not a new idea and has its roots in English Common Law. In its simplest form, it is exclusive monopoly guarantee for 20 years that no one can utilize your stated technology without your approval.

CHAPTER 10   THE ROLE OF TECHNOLOGY

Beyond this, it becomes important to see what can be done to assure the protection of the ideas (intellectual property) that allows the initiator to establish their ownership. With roots in English Common Law, intellectual property laws embrace patents and copyrights. In its most basic form, a patent is an exclusive monopoly granted by the government to an inventor or author. It protects them from infringement and use by others. In its detail, it delineates the idea and how the idea was reduced to practice and includes detailed drawings on its method of operation. Some might argue that publishing that level of detail is an invitation for others to copy and possibly improve on the idea. This must be weighed against the protection the grant affords.

The risk/reward aspect of this can be mitigated using proprietary information. Instead of publishing detailed information in patents and copyrights, certain information is deemed proprietary and protected by secrecy. Coca-Cola is a great example of this. Even with worldwide manufacture and distribution of its products, the original formula has limited availability to its employees and is secured in a safe in the basement of the company's headquarters in Atlanta, GA. At the peak of its life cycle, Polaroid Corporation, the Cambridge, MA, manufacturer of "instant" photography, employed 16,000 employees. It has been noted that only three employees (including the founder, Edwin Land), knew the entire technical process. The rest of the employees worked on the components. Many projects employ a hybrid approach whereby critical elements remain proprietary while others are buffered by patent and copyright protection.

An alternative approach is by securing protection of internal technology or manufacturing processes and resorting to marketing strategies that provide the security of market share. This has been referred to as a "taillight theory." The velocity of entry into a given field provides enough distance to confront competition and thus allows others to only see your taillights.

CHAPTER 10   THE ROLE OF TECHNOLOGY

Were the exposures of information surrounding intellectual property requiring significant care not formidable enough; there is the matter of cost. A basic utility patent costs about $25,000 and requires sustaining fees throughout the 20-year life of the document. International filings can cost about $125,000 per patent. Crafting a patent or copyright requires a skilled patent attorney. Small variations of claim text can significantly alter the value of the document.

Investment

To sustain a strong technological position, a sustaining investment plan must be made. There are two types of investment:

- **Variable costs** such as salaries and ongoing expenses. These expenses are booked in the SGA portion of the income statement. They are also expressed as percentage of revenue. This number allows "comparable" percentages in similar companies and industry standards. It is significant that they be sustained irrespective of fluctuations in the revenue and profitability of the organization.

- **Fixed costs** such as equipment and physical plant (labs) viewed from the Balance Sheet and can be amortized over a period. They also become candidates for loans and mortgage instruments and thus can be spread over time. Only the interest and carrying costs are registered on the income statement. For a long time, it was in vogue to erect impressive R & D centers to help attract talent to positive environments. Route 1 in Central New Jersey is certainly an example of this. This trend seems to decrease. More attention is being focused on internal environments.

CHAPTER 10   THE ROLE OF TECHNOLOGY

Perhaps the most challenging aspect of technology investments is the acquisition and sustainment of talent to maintain the programs. Keeping them relevant implies additional expenses like education and trade show presence.

Innovation and Culture

Sustaining a technical environment that is nimble, adaptable, forward-looking, and willing to absorb risk is a significant challenge. Being "nimble" has become a marker for successful companies. Innovation and its exploitation seem to be a key value element. Among its benefits is that innovative organizations seem to embrace both risk and progressive things more effectively.

There is an example of this in the 3M Company headquartered in St. Paul, MN. It is certainly known for its adhesive-based products; but there is an anecdotal story that seems to capture their sense of innovation. It seems that a production batch of adhesive did not meet internal specifications. At best, it could only be used for small pieces of paper. They were about to discard the batch when an administrative assistant intervened and said it would be useful to have small pieces of removable paper for her notes. Today, we call that multimillion product family as "Post-its." If the organization did not value nimble, innovative applications, that story might not have occurred.

There is yet another dimension to the application of technology. It is the rate of change to the technology. Twenty years ago, Gordon Moore who was one of the founders of Intel Corporation observed that computer memory was evolving at an accelerating rate. With more chip (transister) memory density, the computer could process more complex steps with less power and small footprints. He argued that with each new generation of microprocessor technology, the memory density would double. The observation was coined Moore's Law and was a standard for almost 20 years.

Thomas Friedman, the noted journalist, wrote a book entitled *Thank You for Being Late* (Farrar, Straus and Giroux, New York, 2016). Its premise was to express his gratitude for a parking garage attendant who asked him for writing advise. During his answer, Friedman observed that he had to stop his normal frantic activity to respond to him. In the process he realized that he was on an increasingly active and accelerating path. He questioned whether the technology-driven paths that he observed could continue its pace… and at what price!

Maintaining an innovative and nimble culture is indeed an art form. Much has been written about an innovation culture and the environment that is required to sustain it. Most of the large accounting and information companies (i.e., McKinsey) have working groups and professional working in the area on behalf of clients. Some common elements appear in the literature. Included are the following:

- Need for corporate support, budgets, and validation of the idea
- Developing listening (versus speaking) skills
- Recognizing support through experimental failures
- Hiring individuals with successful experience in the culture
- Steering the organization's business model to areas that are mindful of the value of the innovation culture.

Were it a simple as a list of favorable attributes and encouragement/resources, there would probably be more companies on an innovative culture list. There is a degree of luck and opportunity recognition that is so much a part of it. Clearly, those companies that do master it will recognize more commercial values from the markets in which they do business.

CHAPTER 11

Risks and Their Mitigation

Inherent to any business endeavor is an assumption of risks and the responsibility to offer mitigation strategies for them. Professionally written business plans and project proposals have in common a delineation of known risks and defined mitigation plans to confront and overcome them. In addition, there are financial and marketplace risks for which we do not develop specific strategies, but we can offset their potential financial impact with Balance Sheet reserves. Over time, the accuracy of the reserve accounting became important. A reserve for bad debt, for example, can achieve accuracy over time as the nature of the customer base becomes better known. Although this strategy is sound, some argue that companies can use it to "hide" profits. Indeed, the accounting profession and the Internal Revenue Service (IRS) have provided guidelines as to how reserves should be handled.

There are two broad categories of risk: One might be defined as general to the industry, environment, or technology a company or projects inhabit. The second are those specific to the organization itself. There is probably a third category of risks that is not known or understood. Each group will be examined.

CHAPTER 11   RISKS AND THEIR MITIGATION

External Risks and Mitigation

Risks that affect a project (or company) from outside include government or industry regulations. Most times these issues are public and are open to involvement by the community of the people affected by them. One example might be the impact of safety, environment, or material selections that are controlled by either federal, local, or governmental agencies. Mitigation suggests involvement in the process by trade organizations or simple lobbying techniques. Becoming a "victim" of regulatory change is simply not an option.

There are a series of risk factors that confront any organization. They might include theft, personal liability, fire, or physical damage. Depending on the industries served, the list tends to be somewhat endless. Some external risks such as warranty charges or bad debt can be confronted by financial reserves on the Balance Sheet where they are financially reserved as a buffer. Others such as those mentioned earlier can be mitigated by purchased insurance contracts, intended to protect and even replace defined damages. Of interest are the categories that are specific to a given endeavor.

In attempts to present a balanced perspective about a business proposal, it is critical that the risk and their mitigation be presented. An example of such a listing is shown in the following:

Risk category	Mitigation alternatives
• Technological change	Family design platform Alternatives that confront change, R & D
• Supply chain fluctuations	Constant monitoring, alternative suppliers
• Customer demographics	Alert market surveys
• Regulatory changes	Trade group, lobbyists
• Competitive changes	Product adaptations, marketing incentives
• Organizational adaptation	Constant review and communication
• Capital insufficiency	Short- and long-erm reviews

CHAPTER 11   RISKS AND THEIR MITIGATION

In their article in the *Sloan Management Review* entitled "Managing Risk to Avoid Supply Chain Breakdown" (Fall, 2004), authors Sunil Chopra and ManMohan S. Sohil focus on the balance of management required to offset supply chain risk. They speak of the management challenge to balance risk mitigation efforts without eroding profit margins. They liken the task to a stockbroker who attempts to reach higher level of profits with management of a stock portfolio decisions. They go further to identify three channels of risk that can affect supply chain efficiency. They include supplier related, internal, and customer related.

In a recent (July 2021) article in *The Seattle Times*, there was a story about a machine manufactured to develop ultradense computer chips. It was manufactured by a Dutch manufacturer called ASML. It utilized advanced ultraviolet sources to achieve the performance. The machines cost $150 million. Of significance is a stated marketing strategy by the company not to sell their equipment to China, which is trying to dominate the world supply of chips. In one sense this decision may not be related to a particular company... but demonstrates the global impact of decisions that can add risk to an individual company.

Risk Mitigation. There are both recognized and unrecognized risk in any commercial venture. Good, forward-looking business proposition (plans) attempts to identify risks and provide options for their mitigation. Within this category are foreseeable and repetitive areas for bad debt or inventory shrinkage, for example. The accounting standards and tax experts allow certain amount of reserves for this. Although it does diminish the amounts of profits that may be taxable, the practice of reserve accounting is still considered a positive business discipline.

CHAPTER 11   RISKS AND THEIR MITIGATION

Capital equipment and even real estate investments tend to have formal risk mitigation in the form of insurance policies and warranties. This is an area that most executives are not as conversant, and they may require outside brokers and vendor-based salespeople to administer.

The area of risk that is not as predictable is that which is unforeseen. There is an array of situations that can challenge an organization that are unpredictable. This quandary challenges another dimension of governance. It is that new metrics of being nimble, adaptive, and representing a willingness to adapt. If the price of lumber created in Africa fluctuates to a furniture maker user in America, they must deal with it even though it is set by others not connected with the organization. It is a risk of doing business. The charge of being nimble, adaptive, etc. also helps companies to change in technology, markets, global competition in a general and positive manner.

In reviewing many business plan proposals, I found that those that presented this information were of higher quality and reflected a more sophisticated leadership team.

CHAPTER 12

Summary

The journey through this text has focused on the value of growth in early-stage entities. The perspective allowed us to examine the functional elements' impact on growth and their overall value contribution. The fascination with early-stage companies and projects was useful because they allow closer focus on impact of the growth formulas than larger, more complex organizations and markets.

Formal valuation is a multidisciplined evaluation process. It attempts to rationalize multiple internal and external factors and then reconcile those inputs into a "value" for the overall enterprise. Formal reviews and formation of forward policies should be part of the dialogue at the senior governance level of the organization. New tools and metrics will be required to encourage this. The tools we have today may be sufficient for transactional activity. New tools and approaches will be required going forward. Certainly, outside agencies and government regulations that set the standards will be part of this dialogue. If there is no other reason for this, the urgency created by accelerating trends of information processing and technology on a global basis creates a basis for change that is current.

The journey through this text allows us to examine some of the functional elements of an organization and how they contribute to the overall value of the enterprise. Still there is not a unifying measure of the overall performance. Outside investors and analysts do some indirect measurement but also struggle for overall ratings. It's no longer a local issue. Global commerce and competition serve to increase the need for better measurements. It is not so much an external issue, but it falls into

CHAPTER 12   SUMMARY

the internal self-awareness. It should be on the agenda of each board meeting or governance function within a company.

If done well, it also offers the opportunity to improve strategic decision-making. It also allows better internal control of the allocation of resources that can lead to more competitive operational decision-making. There is little downside.

APPENDIX A

Before You Initiate, Investigate

A Visual Prelaunch Checklist

By Shlomo Maital and Eliezer Shein[*]

> *It is more important to know some of the questions, than to know all of the answers.*
>
> —James Thurber, American author

Introduction

How can businesses grow their "top line" (revenue) and bottom lines (gross profit, operating profit, and net profit)? The preceding chapters by Jerome Schaufeld offer pragmatic, proven tools.

In this Appendix, we focus on the birth of a new product or service, or a new venture, and suggest ways to improve the chances of establishing the preconditions of viable sustained growth, by navigating an exhaustive protocol or checklist. This protocol helps innovators decide how and whether the "embryo" can become a viable, thriving, vigorous, growing business.

---

[*]Senior research fellows, S. Neaman Institute for National Policy Research, Technion-Israel Institute of Technology

APPENDIX A BEFORE YOU INITIATE, INVESTIGATE

According to the late Harvard Business School professor Clayton Christensen, there are over 30,000 new products introduced every year, and 95% fail. And as the late great management consultant Peter Drucker cautioned, businesses fail not because they do things wrong – but because they do the wrong things [3].

Hence, if innovation is indeed the core driver of corporate growth, for startups and giant multinationals alike, we must ask, following Christensen and Drucker, *why do businesses do the wrong things?*

A report by the Israel Venture Center, studying 10,000 Israeli startups from 1997 through 2014, reveals this: "Only four of 100 startups succeed; only four of 500 are successful growing independently" [2]. Why then do some 95% of new product launches fail, and 96% of Israeli startups?

We suggest the answer lies in perhaps two unlikely places – in a hospital and on the tarmac of a busy commercial airport.

In hospitals, it has been shown that use of protocols – precisely defined rules to be followed when doing a medical procedure or in fact any process requiring rigor and precision – saves money and, more importantly, saves lives.

At airports, we doubt anyone would board a commercial airliner, unless they knew that the pilot and copilot had gone through a careful detailed checklist, including a walk-around the aircraft for visual inspection.[1]

Why, then, have so many startup launches, and new product launches, failed to employ similar protocols, failed to ask in advance the right questions, and, hence, sadly, crashed and burnt? Why do

---

[1] "We begin the flight deck setup, verifying each switch and lever is in the proper position. One pilot then goes outside to visually inspect the airplane. The walk-around is done before each flight looking for leaks, bird strikes or anything else unusual. The ramp is often busy with tugs, baggage carts, fuel trucks and belt loaders. It can be a hazardous place, particularly during inclement weather. Bags and freight are going up the belt loader and into the holds. Passengers are boarding as the walk-around ends. It's then back into the flight deck to continue with the preparations...." www.usatoday.com/story/travel/columnist/cox/2018/08/19/standard-pilot-procedure-starting-flight/1009100002/

innovators not ask the standard set of questions that can help avoid failure? Why do many innovators not engage in a metaphoric "walk-around" that no pilot would ever dismiss?

In this brief chapter, we propose a visual quantitative dashboard based on seven basic sets of questions. They can alert innovators and entrepreneurs to potential fatal weaknesses in their concepts, hopefully in time to forestall or repair them.

Some claim that high failure rates are inevitable in high-risk startups and product launches. We believe that a substantial portion of those failure rates are eminently preventable, using best-practice prelaunch protocols. In a study of Technion – Israel Institute of Technology graduates who went on to launch startups, we found that a large percentage did not study in any fashion aspects of business and management during their undergraduate years [4].

A Framework to Investigate, Then Initiate

Table A-1 provides a matrix, or a framework, for conducting a thorough prelaunch investigation of a new product or service idea or a business concept for a startup. We propose organizing the prelaunch protocol based on eight "hard" tangible business issues and seven "soft" intangible areas.

The tangible areas, the rows of the critical success factors matrix, are understanding current and future markets; understanding your products and services; people: team building, cultivation and retention; innovation and adaptation to change; strategy, planning and execution; finance and investment; understanding risk, reward and uncertainty; and cash management. If you have cash, you can procure the vital things you need. If you lack cash, you are forced to compromise, improvise, or do without vital skills and resources. Note: Many or all of these topics are covered at length in the preceding chapters in this book and in Schaufeld [6].

The intangible (soft) areas, the columns of the matrix, are relationships, knowledge, leadership and communication, culture and values, reputation and trust, skills and competencies, and processes and systems (meritocracy).

Each cell in the 8x7 matrix embodies the interaction of a tangible business area and an intangible business area. *And behind each cell, we have developed an exhaustive list of evaluative questions, each of which requires a score between 1 and 5.* The ultimate goal is to create a visual dashboard depiction of the concept, quantified, and to thus identify potential weaknesses.

Figure A-1 provides an example of such a visualization of an investigative protocol. What it shows is a product, or a startup, with relatively strong (demonstrated) market need, a reasonably strong team, and very strong business model – but very weak sales and marketing, mediocre customer intimacy, a paucity of cash, and perhaps mediocre product "wow." This dashboard predicts failure due to lack of cash and poor sales and marketing. Chances of success improve markedly should these two lacunae be remedied – *in advance*. They can of course be repaired after launch – but this is much more difficult.

Case Study: Better Place[2]

Better Place was perhaps Israel's most spectacular – and perhaps predictable – failure. It was founded by Shai Agassi, a brilliant successful software engineer and entrepreneur, in 2008, to sell electric cars whose depleted electric batteries could be quickly and robotically exchanged for fully charged ones. More than $900 m was invested.

---

[2] See Maital & Shein [5].

The company declared bankruptcy in May 2013. Why?

- People: No one in senior management had experience in the automobile industry. And there was cronyism everywhere.
- Cash: With coffers overflowing, spending was frivolous and excessive. "Cash pollution" is how we describe this, as a rare case of having too much money rather than too little.
- Mismanagement: Not understanding the market.
- Bloated workforce: By August 2012, the company employed 560 people and 200 contract workers!
- Product: The Renault Fluence was clunky, stodgy, and unpopular with Israelis. The promised ubiquitous charging stations never happened.

These are some of the issues that could have been solved very early in the project timeline.

We believe an investigative 8x7 dashboard, carefully constructed in advance, could have revealed at least some of the ultimately fatal flaws in the Better Place concept. At the least, had it been used, someone with automotive industry experience might have been put in place from the outset.

Conclusion

We have field-tested our protocol on a number of startups. In truth, it proved somewhat annoying. To entrepreneurs, flushed with the drama, romance, and excitement of a radical new product launch, it is tedious and tiresome to be forced to work through a long list of questions and, worse, to quantify answers to each. And for highly intelligent entrepreneurs who are laser-focused on their unique technology, frankly, the humdrum business aspects are somewhat irritating.

The Bible speaks of a future time of world peace when the wolf will lie down with the lamb. For companies seeking growth through innovation, this is the dilemma. The wolf is the fierce and wild creativity driving the innovation process. The lamb is the discipline, rigor, and methodical management needed to achieve sustained, consistent growth. Can they coexist and collaborate? They can. They must!

We hope and trust that an exhaustive investigative protocol can help bold innovators think through their creative ideas, systematically, and put all the needed pieces in place, or most of them, before launch.

All too often, the sequence is "initiate – then investigate." Let us put the horse before the cart and investigate, *then* initiate – as common-sense business practice. Let us pilot our launches as experienced commercial pilots do before takeoff.

References

[1] Heymann T. Clinical protocols are key to quality health care delivery. Int J Health Care Qual Assur. 1994;7(7):14-7.

[2] Israel Venture Center. "Israel Startup Success Report." Tel Aviv, 2015.

[3] Drucker, Peter. "Theory of Business." Harvard Business Review, Sept.-Oct. 1994.

APPENDIX A BEFORE YOU INITIATE, INVESTIGATE

[4] Buchnik, Tsipy, Vered Gilad, and Shlomo Maital. "UNIVERSITIES' INFLUENCE ON STUDENT DECISIONS TO BECOME ENTREPRENEURS: THEORY AND EVIDENCE." Journal of Entrepreneurship Education 21.3 (2018): 1-19.

[5] S. Maital, E. Shein. "A Broken Place: The Spectacular Failure of the Startup That was Going to Change the World But Failed in a Big Way." S. Neaman Institute, Technion, 2017.

[6] Schaufeld, Jerry. "Commercializing Innovation." Turning Technology Breakthroughs into Products. New York: Apress (2015).

Table A-1. *An 8x7 Matrix for Investigating Before Initiating*

Enterprise Assessment Tool			Startup or SME Company Name			
Critical Success Factors			Critical Success Factors		Critical Success Factors	

The following matrix describes the 49 Critical Success Factors (CSFs) which are critical to the success of the enterprise.
The CSFs are determined by checking a Real Business Issue against an Intangible Soft Area.

Critical Success Factors		Intangible Soft Area 1 — Relationships	Intangible Soft Area 2 — Knowledge	Intangible Soft Area 3 — Leadership and Communication	Intangible Soft Area 4 — Culture and Values	Intangible Soft Area 5 — Reputation and Trust	Intangible Soft Area 6 — Skills and Competencies	Intangible Soft Area 7 — Processes and Systems (Meritocracy)
Tangible Real Business Issues	1. Understanding Current and Future Markets	Strength of channels and ability to access chosen markets	Accuracy and relevance of our market research and intelligence. Define the unmet need in the market	Pragmatic and sustainable direction and focus	Negotiating power and influence with suppliers & collaborators	Delivering our promises on time and to specification	Understanding of factors which drive market attractiveness	Focus on need for continual improvement in all we do
	2. Understanding Your Products and Services	Working with others to develop customer solutions	Relative attractiveness of features and benefits	Prioritization of market research and product development	Customer loyalty based on quality of experiences	Our solutions set the standard for value and performance	Effective use of design covering the whole of each product's life	Fit between production capabilities and market needs
	3. People: Team Building, Cultivation and Retention	Excellence in networking teamwork and collaboration	Getting the right mix of wisdom and experience to succeed	Efforts aligned towards a shared aim and purpose	Motivating by rewarding productive behaviours	Understanding implications and consequences of ways of working	Training, development and learning opportunities	Staff appraisal is linked to critical success factors
	4. Innovation and Adaptation to Change	Development of sensors and early warning systems	Development of proprietary solutions and valuable Intellectual Property Rights (IPR)	Effective trade off between current and future needs	Listening to and sharing ideas with others to build solutions	Sensitivity in dealing with problems and concerns	Ability to see problems and opportunities in true context	Effective processes for making best use of good ideas
	5. Strategy, Planning and Execution	Negotiating strength within the value chain	Strength of management track record to date	We set realistic objectives for each of our key activities	Changes which we implement create value for stakeholders	We are viewed as a safe and trust worthy by those we work with	We prioritize actions based on both importance and urgency	We understand interconnections & dependencies between actions
	6. Finance and Investment	Ability to build and convey an attractive Value Proposition	Pricing and budgeting strategies are based on actual evidence	Determination to succeed despite obstacles and difficulties	We take a pragmatic view in terms of sharing rewards	Open and honest dialogue with financiers and partners	Ability of the business to grow and to generate profits	Control of all operations and in particularly cash flow
	7. Understanding Risk, Reward & Uncertainty	Considering scenarios helps us to live with uncertainty	We have metrics which accurately keep track of all our CSF's	We have routines and frameworks for delegation and control	We work with our stakeholders to limit areas of dissatisfaction	Retaining the support needed to survive temporary setbacks	Speed with which we learn from mistakes and act to correct them	Ability to understand risks and applying the needed operations for managing them
	8. Cash Management	Raising capital is important. Creating good relations with VCs by building trust.	Cash is the lifeblood of the company. We understand the process of cash management.	We communicate well with the financial market.	Many start-ups and SMEs fail due to poor cash management. So we make sure we keep Operating Expenses Under Control, and Control the cash flow very carefully.	Trust and Integrity are very important. Funders want to know that!	A great CFO is distinguished by his or her experience in the field. It is our understanding that the CFO must have high-level operational experience and financial experience. Our CFO must have skills in forward-looking strategies.	We make sure we use state-of-the-art technology
		1 Intangible Soft Area	2 Intangible Soft Area	3 Intangible Soft Area	4 Intangible Soft Area	5 Intangible Soft Area	6 Intangible Soft Area	7 Intangible Soft Area

APPENDIX A   BEFORE YOU INITIATE, INVESTIGATE

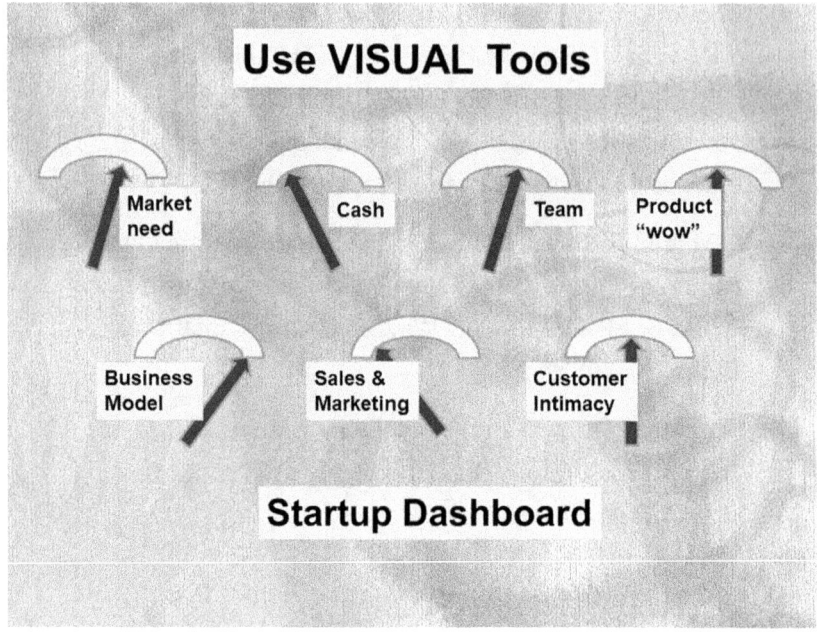

Figure A-1. An "Investigate, Then Initiate" Dashboard

Index

A

Accounts Payable, 54, 55
Adhesive-based products, 90
American Research and Development Corporation (ARDC), 59
Angel Capital Association (ACA), 58, 78
Angel (individual) investors, 78
Automobiles, 85
Average selling price (ASP), 39

B

Balance Sheet, 53–55, 63
Bottom-up approach, 66, 81
Break-even model, 62
Business plans, 42, 74, 93

C

Capital equipment, 8, 31, 96
Cash management, 24, 56, 100
Chief Executive Officer (CEO), 11
Chief financial officer (CFO), 62, 82
C-level management, 15, 67
Cohesive models, 42
Commercial entities, 2
Communication, 43, 46, 83
Conventional business, 41
Conventional organization, 44
Corporate entities, 65
Corporate-level decisions, 69
Critical resources
   financial, 68
   human, 68
   plant and equipment/automation, 69
Currency fluctuations, 22, 31
Current Ratio, 55

D

Decision-making, 15, 66, 98
Defense Advanced Research Projects Agency (DARPA), 76
Digital economy, 15
Digital Equipment Corporation (DEC), 60

INDEX

E

Early-stage capital, 62
Empowering leadership, 67
Engineering organizational resources, 51
Entrepreneurial mindset, 16
Equity-based investments, 77
Equity infusions, 52

F

Family-run models, 57
Financial capital, 9, 51
Financial markets, 56, 57
Financial metrics, 80
Financial resources, 62
Financial tools, 53
Forecast models, 8
Formal documents, 37

G

General Motors, 44
Geopolitical forces, 32
Global commerce, 97
Global economies, 63
Global indicators, 35
Governance model, 38
Greiner Curve, 47–49
Gross domestic product (GDP), 29

H

Hierarchal model, 43, 68

I, J, K

IBM Rule of Six, 67
Incentive (mis)alignment risk, 42
Individual Angel investors, 78
Information risk, 42
Initial capitalization, 25
Innovation, 86, 90
Intellectual property (IP), 5
Intellectual protection, 87
Internal Revenue Service (IRS), 93
Internal technology, 88
Investment firm, 59
Investment plan, 89
    fixed costs, 89
    variable costs, 89

L

Local economies, 28
Long-term economic indicators, 33
Lopsided valuations, 52
Lumber index, 30, 33

M

Macroeconomic indicators, 29
Market-based external transaction, 31
Marketing, 71
    function, 12, 71, 73, 74
    process, 71, 72
Mergers and acquisitions (M & A), 69

Metrics, 39
Microprocessor, 86

N

National Science Foundation (NSF), 76
Net Income/Loss, 55
Non-dilutive cash, 52
Non-dilutive investment, 78
Non-dilutive mechanisms, 62
Non-equity sources, 5
Not-for-profit organizations, 2

O

Organizational environment, 67
Organizational growth, 10, 47

P, Q

Platform design technology, 7
Prelaunch protocol, 101

R

Return on investment (ROI), 77, 80
Risks, mitigation, 94, 95
Rule of Six model, 46

S

"S" Curve, 3, 46, 49
    capital, 9
    central focus, 8
    digital economy, 15, 16
    disruption, 14, 15
    domain, 4
    external focus, 5
    external issues/competition, 12, 13
    growth, 9
    human resources, 9
    issues, 7
    market-centered issues, 11
    organization, 10
    post-sales opportunities, 13
    technology, 9
    transfer function, 6
Series A events, 79
Service-based operations, 63
Shareholder interests, 65
Shareholder's Equity, 54
Small Business Innovation Research (SBIR), 76
Sources of information, 81
Stock dilution, 57

T

Taillight theory, 88
Talent
    attract, 45
    sources, 45
Technology-based companies, 58
Technology-based ventures, 59
Top-down approach, 66

INDEX

Transactions, 16
Transfer function, 6

U
University of Southern California (USC), 47

V, W, X, Y, Z
Valuation analytics, 40
Venture capital, 78

GPSR Compliance
The European Union's (EU) General Product Safety Regulation (GPSR) is a set of rules that requires consumer products to be safe and our obligations to ensure this.

If you have any concerns about our products, you can contact us on

ProductSafety@springernature.com

In case Publisher is established outside the EU, the EU authorized representative is:

Springer Nature Customer Service Center GmbH
Europaplatz 3
69115 Heidelberg, Germany

www.ingramcontent.com/pod-product-compliance
Lightning Source LLC
LaVergne TN
LVHW010344260326
834688LV00036B/871